SELKIRK

by

Robin Mathews

Steel Rail Educational Publishing
P.O. Box 6813, Station A
Toronto, Ontario
M5W 1X6

ALGOMA COLLEGE LIBRARY

Steel Rail Educational Publishing

Publishing for the People

Steel Rail Educational Publishing is incorporated as a corporation without share capital and is run by the Steel Rail Collective.

The main thrust of Steel Rail is to search for and publish books written by Canadians, about Canada and the Canadian people's struggles throughtout their history, and international titles of interest and value. Steel Rail is a house through which people can exchange ideas and publish materials that might not otherwise be published.

Canadian Catalogue in Publication Data

Mathews, Robin, 1931
  Selkirk

(Canadian historical plays ; no. 1 ISSN 0702-388X)
ISBN 0-88791-008-4 pa.

1. Red River Settlement, Man. - Drama. I. Title. II. Series.

PS8526.A85S44   C812'.5'4   C77-001541-7
PR9199.3.M38S44

Introduction

Selkirk was first produced at the Alumni Theatre of Carleton University as a joint production of The Great Canadian Theatre Company and the Carleton University Fine Arts Committee, October 28, 29, 30, 31 and November 4, 5, 6, 7, 1976, and was directed by Larry McDonald.

An historial play, Selkirk covers a ten year period and several thousands of miles. In order to provide for rapid movement and continuity of action a three-level set was designed (see illustrations). On three levels action can be fast, and the passage of time can be suggested effectively. Scenes were bridged often by the use of a flute and a mouth organ. The passage from the Old World to the New was underscored by a shift in instrument and in tempo and type of melody.

The set was unadorned. Decor was all movable. Costume and properties were used to signify places as different as wealthy Old World interiors and the ramparts of a North West Company fort.

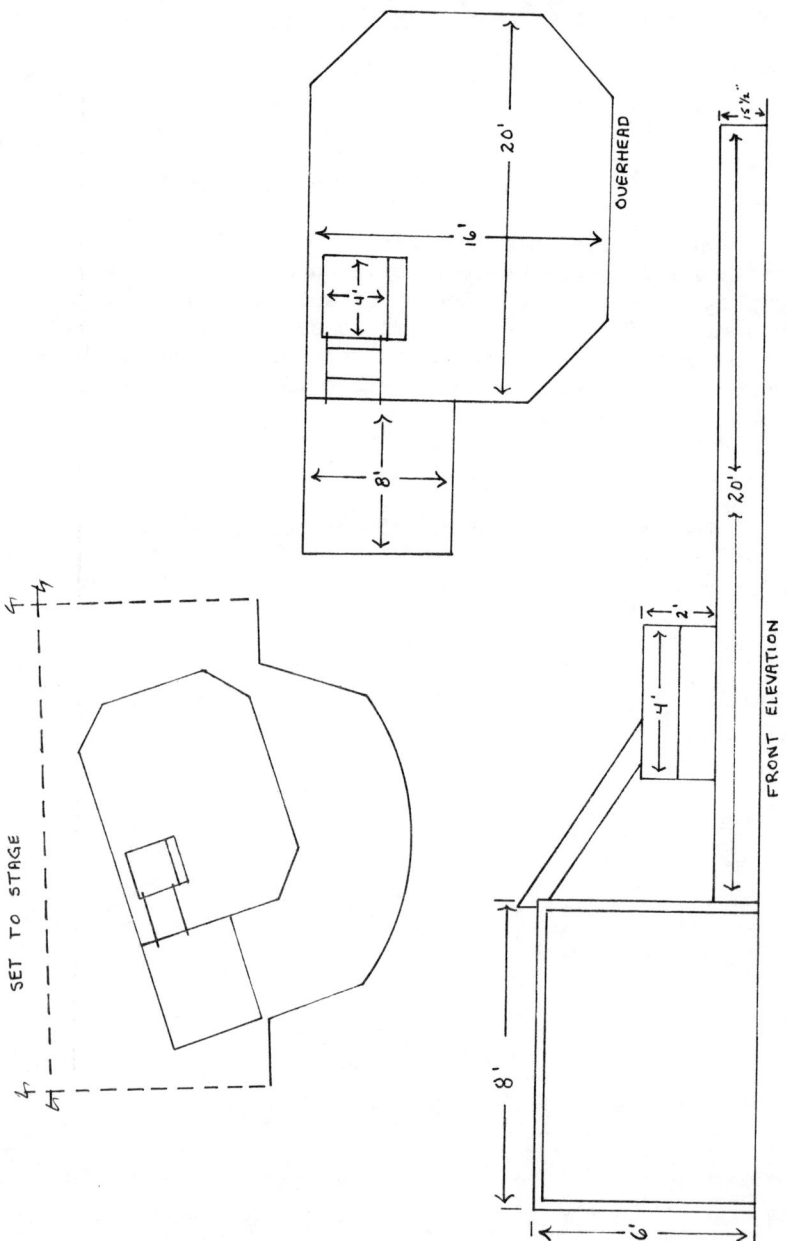

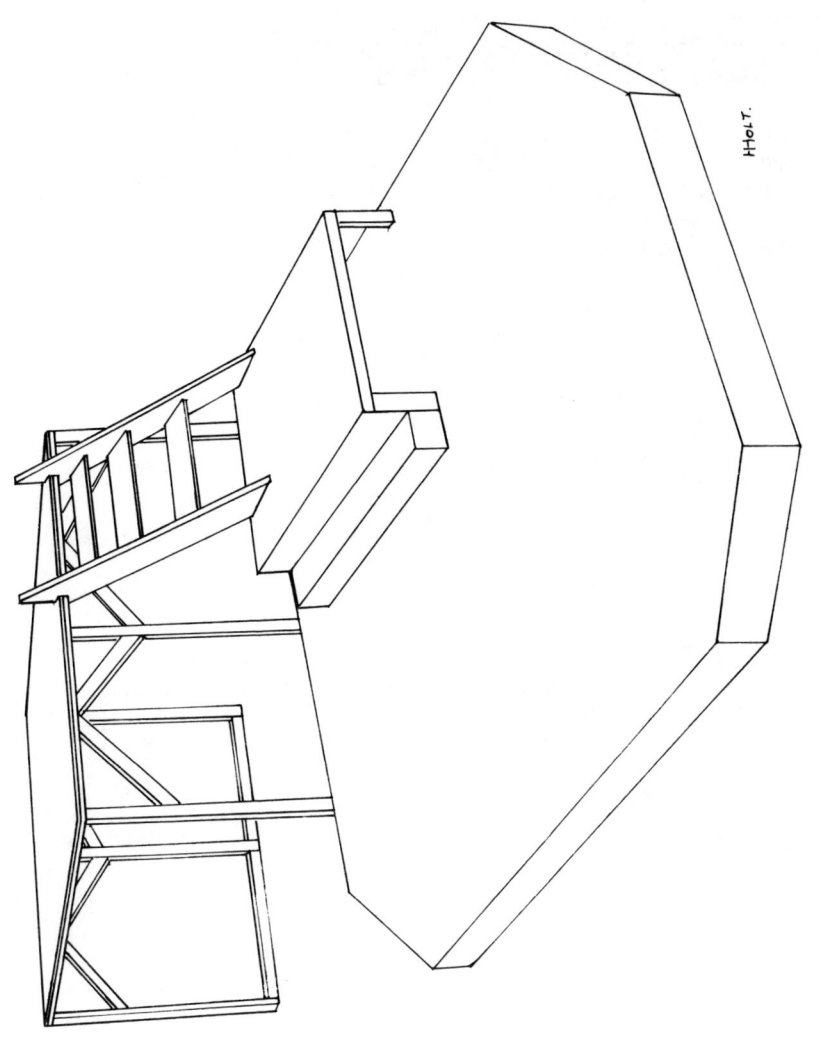

Scene Division

Scene One	1811	London
Scene Two	1811	London
Scene Three	1814	North West
Scene Four	1814	Fort William
Scene Five	1815	Fort Gibraltar
Scene Six	1815	Attack on Fort
Scene Seven	1815	Chateau de Ramezay
Scene Eight	1815	Fort William
Scene Nine	1815	Fort William
Scene Ten	1815	Fort William
Scene Eleven	1816	The Rondelay
Scene Twelve	1817	Trials
Scene Thirteen	1818	Montreal
Scene Fourteen	1818	Trial
Scene Fifteen	1818	Montreal
Scene Sixteen	1820	London
Scene Seventeen	1821	North West

Set Drawings by Helen Holt.

All photographs courtesy of John Bingham, Ottawa.

Tim O,Ray as Duncan Cameron, Bill Walther as William MacGillivray. <u>Planning to stop the Selkirk Settlement.</u> (Scene Four).

David Hudson as Alexander MacDonald, Hal Wake as Sheriff Spencer and Barry Burns as a North West Company employee. <u>The Arrest of Sheriff Spencer.</u> (Scene Five).

Hal Wake as Sheriff Spencer, Michael Thompson as George Campbell, David Hudson as Alexander MacDonald. First news of Metis attack. (Scene Five).

David Hudson as Alexander MacDonald, Douglas Cowan as John Halkett, Bill Walther as William MacGillivray, Barry Burns as Sergeant McNab. Occupation of Fort William. (Scene Eight).

Douglas Cowan as John Halkett, Bill Walther as William MacGillivray. The occupation of Fort William. (Scene Eight).

Douglas Campbell as Lord Selkirk, Mary Neville as Lady Selkirk. Crisis at Fort William. (Scene Nine).

Bill Walther as William MacGillivray, Michael Thompson as Lord Sherbrooke. <u>Asking for action against the settlers</u>. (Scene Eleven).

Douglas Campbell as Lord Selkirk. <u>Punishment by trial</u>. (Scene Twelve).

Cast in order of appearance

```
Lord Selkirk........................Douglas Campbell
Halkett.............................Douglas Cowan
Macdonnell..........................David Potter
McLoughlin..........................Geoff Bowie
Lady Selkirk........................Mary Neville
MacGillivray........................Bill Walther
Cameron.............................Tim O'Ray
Pritchard...........................Carlos Vieira
MacDonald, Robinson.................David Hudson
Campbell, Sherbrooke................Michael Thompson
Sheriff Spencer,
Chief Justice Powell................Hal Wake
Fort Prostitute.....................Susan Seymour
Sergeant McNab......................Barry Burns
Bathurst............................Sean McCutcheon
Judges..............................Geoff Bowie,
                                    Carlos Vieira
                                    Hal Wake

Music...............................Sean McCutcheon
Song of Nor'Westers.................Tim O'Ray
```

Directed by: Larry McDonald

Set Design: Helen Holt, Mike Schmidt

Lighting Design: Mike Schmidt

ACT I

Scene One: Britain. Lord Selkirk's home.

Time: 1811.

SELKIRK:
    Miles Macdonnell, you have been here before with similar stories. You heat too quickly. You jump too quickly to your weapons man.

MACDONNELL:
    With respect my lord. I have to disagree. I know the New World.

SELKIRK:
    That's why I made you governor of Assiniboia and the colony to be.

MACDONNELL:
    You must permit me...

SELKIRK:
    Oh, I permit you what you need, Mr. Macdonnell. And I shall continue to do so. But you let a little story in the Inverness Journal pitch you into a great state, do you not?

MACDONNELL:
    It's lies and slanders of this kind that are hurting us. Recruiting for the colony slows. It even goes backwards.

SELKIRK:
    It's only a newspaper report. What do you think of it, John?

HALKETT:
    Well now. It's a pack of damned lies, skillfully put together. Slanderous damnation of the colonization scheme...signed if you like by a former settler in the Northwest. Apart from that I suppose it's harmless enough. Probably very good journalism, otherwise.

MACDONNELL:
You may joke, John Halkett. A former settler indeed. It's William MacGillivray himself, I'll bet, offering himself as settler and colonist recently returned.

SELKIRK:
Come, come Mr. Macdonnell. It could be a real returned settler you know. Many a one wants a palatial country estate handed him in the midst of a thriving city in the New World.

MACDONNELL:
You may jest, too, my lord. But you'd better not sell MacGillivray and the North West Company short.

SELKIRK:
The North West Company has always been, even before my grant, a lawless interloper on chartered and granted Hudson's Bay territory. Is that not so, John? Is it not simple, legal fact?

HALKETT:
Yes, Thomas, it is so. A simple legal fact. We have absolute right on our side. They have on the other hand, possession and quite long customary use. They possess nothing in law. But they do possess a thriving business that stretches right across the land we intend to settle. A business, by the way, that makes a lot of coffers clink in London town as well as in Montreal.

MACDONNELL:
They won't move aside for a piece of paper. That's what the newstory means. But don't pay me any heed. I've brought one of the settlers with me. Will you talk to him?

SELKIRK:
We will happily. Show him in Mr. Macdonnell.

MACDONNELL:
My lord, Mr. Halkett, this is Paul McLoughlin who

has signed up as a settler for the first voyage across to the New World. Five or six of his friends also signed up, but they've been frightened away. And not just by a newspaper story.

SELKIRK:
Mr. McLoughlin, Mr. Macdonnell tells me you have some doubts about the colony.

MCLOUGHLIN:
I have not doubts, my lord. I want to go. I need to go to the New World if I'm to have any future.

SELKIRK:
You find the contract's fair?

MCLOUGHLIN:
The contract's fair as any I've heard of, more fair. But the Nor'Westers have spread stories in every tavern and shop that it's killing cold, a barren land full of bloodthirsty savages.

SELKIRK:
Is that all, those fantasy stories?

MCLOUGHLIN:
No, my lord. They encourage us to break our contracts and keep the money you've already paid us.

MACDONNELL:
They've even got some to contract under false names and then withdraw to rob you of money.

SELKIRK:
Is that all to the story?

MCLOUGHLIN:
No it isn't my lord.

MACDONNELL:
They've beaten a number of the contracted men so badly they can't travel.

SELKIRK:
 Is that true, Mr. McLoughlin? Is that what happened to you?

MCLOUGHLIN:
 It's not as simple as that, my lord.

SELKIRK:
 Then how is it?

MCLOUGHLIN:
 Well who's to say how a tavern brawl starts, and who's to say who strikes the first blow? But there's many a brawl where the colonists drink. We've been much beaten, I fear.

SELKIRK:
 But that's sheer ruffianism. When MacGillivray and Cameron came to the Company meeting, they were gentlemen, no doubt of that. As a...

MACDONNELL:
 Excuse me my lord, the North West Company rules the land in the West with a pack of ruffians and a force of arms. You're only seeing a hint of their tactics here...

SELKIRK:
 Miles Macdonnell, the settling of a colony of good men and women who've been driven from their lands in Scotland and Ireland will not be obstructed by the violence of a pack of ruffians. We shall take law and order with us. We are law and order. The North West Company is illegally on Hudson's Bay Company grant lands. The grant to me, within Hudson's Bay lands is clearly drawn, legally granted, fully recorded.

MACDONNELL:
 You are talking about grants and pieces of paper again.

SELKIRK:
> Mr. Macdonnell, I am empowered to make a colony.
> The colony of the Red River will be a great piece
> of history, gentlemen, a great beginning...Come.
> Have some vision. We will lift the poor, exploited
> lowly folk of this land onto British lands in the
> New World where they will flourish for the good of
> Britain and for themselves.

HALKETT:
> Touching poetry, Thomas. But do you see us simply
> carrying law and order with us like a paper pro-
> clamation into the Indian country, ruled as it is
> by assassins and thugs? Do you think it will hold
> off the likes of Duncan Cameron and William
> MacGillivray?

MACDONNELL:
> I certainly don't.

SELKIRK:
> How then will you keep the peace, Governor
> Macdonnell? Do you intend to enter a common trade
> war such as we are asked to witness regularly in
> the rebel colonies now called the United States?
> Do you intend to take a government army, as they
> do, and wipe out the native peoples? We're bad
> sir, I'll admit, but we don't stoop to that level
> of state policy. Shall we send settlers or an
> army of occupation?

MACDONNELL:
> I'll follow your orders to the letter, my lord, as
> you well know. But a governor has to govern, has
> to have leeway to act. All I ask is that you know
> the enemy.

SELKIRK:
> I still think you go in haste. We have the land
> on legal purchase. We hold all the cards. We
> have the active cooperation of the Hudson's Bay
> Company. And on top of all that we are doing
> something the government of Great Britain is

watching with genuine interest.

MACDONNELL:
> I don't know what the men in government are saying, but everyone else is saying you're a romantic murderer. You'll take the settlers, they say, into the same suicide you took them to in Prince Edward Island and the Baldoon colony of Upper Canada.

SELKIRK:
> My God, they are doing a job, aren't they. The Prince Edward Island experiment is fast becoming a symbol of all that can be done with colonization. And the money I've pumped into Baldoon would bankrupt most of my critics a thousand times over...

HALKETT:
> They say you personally denied money the colonists needed, withheld good land, and let them die like flies to save yourself a penny.

MACDONNELL:
> The slanders of Cameron and MacGillivray have been effective my lord.

SELKIRK:
> To save myself a penny? What vicious, slanderous rogues. But we mustn't stoop to their slander and methods. We have a job to do, to prove that ordinary folk are not possessions but responsible creatures with the right to seek honourable and dignified lives. We shall plant those ideas in the New World, in Canada. The North West Company can't stop us with slander or with force because we have the law on our side. And we have history on our side too, a greater power even than the law. We won't make war. We will meet slander with firmness, savagery with the law consistently applied.

(Enter Lady Selkirk)

LADY SELKIRK:
> Here's a serious set of faces. Good afternoon Mr. Macdonnell. I must remind you, Thomas, that we are expected this evening, and the Duke does not appreciate late arrivers. I've just received a note to say the guest list has been expanded to include two gentlemen lately arrived from the Canadas, a Mr. Duncan Cameron and a Mr. William MacGillivray. That should prove an evening to remember.

MACDONNELL:
> You remind us, my lady of our duties. Mr. McLoughlin here is going to help Mr. Halkett and me track down some of the people bribing and threatening our colonists.

HALKETT:
> Come along then. Let's get about that business.

(Macdonnell and Halkett go out with McLoughlin to whom Lord Selkirk speaks, calling him back)

SELKIRK:
> Mr. McLoughlin...

MCLOUGHLIN:
> My lord...

SELKIRK:
> I'm happy you came here, Mr. McLoughlin, and I know you'll stay true to the colony. I'm not saying it'll be easy, but I believe there's much to hope for. There's a future there for you.

MCLOUGHLIN:
> We'll build a colony there if it's up to me. I'm not afraid.

SELKIRK:
> Good man, Paul McLoughlin. If I don't see you again here, I'll see you in the New World. Good luck man. Good luck.

(McLoughlin leaves)

LADY SELKIRK:
>   What's brother John up to? What's all this talk about bribery and threatening?

SELKIRK:
>   He and Mcdonnell are chasing after some rumours about savagery among the Nor'Westers.

LADY SELKIRK:
>   More of that Thomas. It makes me uneasy. The Northwest seems so far off. Supply lines, everything, will be strung out so. Even the map of it makes my head spin.

SELKIRK:
>   We've an adversary out there who wants to make trouble. We'll have to circle and circle him without striking. It'll be hard.

LADY SELKIRK:
>   I don't like the uncertainty in this venture.

SELKIRK:
>   Oh, there's something in the rumour, but it's overblown.

LADY SELKIRK:
>   The rumour heightens, talk of savagery, talk of violence. Your health Thomas, don't forget that ...The first ship hasn't left yet.

SELKIRK:
>   Well?

LADY SELKIRK:
>   We could withdraw from this one...

SELKIRK:
>   Could we?

LADY SELKIRK:
>   I don't mean from colonization, but from this kind.

LADY SELKIRK (cont'd)
> Can you manage the strain of it? Is it worth it? There'll be other chances. And you've been so well these past years. Maybe we shouldn't press our luck...

SELKIRK:
> For a mere ten shillings we've been granted a territory to open that's bigger than this whole country. We can't go back now. And we don't have to. Oh, the Nor'Westers will bluster and gesture and puff and shout some to scare us off. But once we're there, once the settlement is on the ground, the bluster'll fade away, because it'll have to. If I didn't think that, I wouldn't send the first shipload. Once they settle in and stories start coming back about the land and the crops, we won't be able to fill ships fast enough.

LADY SELKIRK:
> You're sure it will all prove out for the good.

SELKIRK:
> I am completely and utterly certain.

LADY SELKIRK:
> Very well, tonight we stay very cool. Cool and sharp, Lord Selkirk. We will deal with Cameron and MacGillivray tonight for the last time if we can do it. When we meet them, we will circle them with our absolute confidence and conviction. We will hypnotize them. All will be well.

(Exit)

Scene Two

(Lights up on stage with MacGillivray and Cameron. From behind, music and the sounds of a party from which they have withdrawn)

MACGILLIVRAY:
    The good Lord Selkirk has brought his fine folk before us to do their cottage entertainments and to show the world their good, simple hearts.

CAMERON:
    Have we travelled from Montreal for this kind of thing, Mr. MacGillivray?

MACGILLIVRAY:
    We're all to be <u>democrats</u> now. He's infected with Robbie Burns and <u>that new</u> man, William Wordsworth. He wants all Britain to find out the good, fair hearts of the simple, smelly peasants.

CAMERON:
    He wants them to fall in love with his half-assed scheme to make himself a lord in two worlds, you mean.

MACGILLIVRAY:
    How vulgar you are Cameron. He wants to release the peasants from their chains. He wants to ship them to a brave new colony where they will build a vaster Britain and a New Jerusalem.

CAMERON:
    Smack in the centre of the fur-trade country. I say damn Wordsworth and his whole democratic crowd. Stop him now, MacGillivray. Surely he can't be such a fool as...

MACGILLIVRAY:
    Maybe you should ask him yourself, Duncan Cameron (MacGillivray has been looking across the stage, sights Selkirk) because he's on his way towards us right now.

MACGILLIVRAY (cont'd)
>Well, well, well, my Lord Selkirk is it? Imagine Mr. Cameron, the triumph of meeting a man being talked about on two continents at least...Or perhaps you have met Mr. Cameron already, my lord, around one of your great and sweeping humanitarian projects?

SELKIRK:
>No, but I saw you both at the last meeting of the Hudson's Bay Company which you were good enough to scamper across the Atlantic to attend...but forgive me, you haven't met my wife or her brother, Mr. John Halkett, I'm sure.

(MacGillivray and Cameron bow to Lady Selkirk with a slight air of mockery)

MACGILLIVRAY:
>My Lady Selkirk's beauty is almost as widely known as is her husband's desire to dabble in dreamy schemes of human salvation.

LADY SELKIRK:
>Colonization of the starving and dispossessed is not a dreamy scheme of human salvation, Mr. MacGillivray, but an act of simple necessity.

SELKIRK:
>Which reminds me. We must seize this opportunity to plan.

MACGILLIVRAY:
>I fear we have little to talk about, my lord.

SELKIRK:
>The colonization plans must interest you, both as the man who runs the North West Company and as a member of the Legislative Council of Upper Canada. We must plan for the new territories together...

MACGILLIVRAY:
>The new territories are not so new my lord...But

even so I fear they are no place to take civilized people. Settlers are not liked by the savage people.

SELKIRK:
We have evidence to prove that is not the case...

MACGILLIVRAY:
Evidence, have you. I deeply regret that you'd think of putting fine and courageous British folk in such danger...I regret that my lord. Your husband, Lady Selkirk, is sending the flower of British peasantry to almost certain death. Can you not dissuade him from it...?

LADY SELKIRK:
You prefer, Mr. MacGillivray, that they should starve to death at home.

HALKETT:
We have a tract of land spreading endlessly away, with soil enough to feed half the world. The Indian people are friendly - we've full reports of that...

SELKIRK:
I think we've heard enough talk of death and starvation and violence.

MACGILLIVRAY:
Sheer romanticism, sheer fantasy to put it simply.

CAMERON:
What a picture, what a picture!

MACGILLIVRAY:
Neither of you has set foot in, neither of you knows the Northwest, the Indian Country as it's called.

SELKIRK:
If properly cultivated, it'll be fine land...

CAMERON:
> For fur-bearing animals and savages. If you can tell them apart. When the country's used liberally and treated well, the savages and the animals and a few tough traders can scratch a living off the land. But that's all.

MACGILLIVRAY:
> Think of it. Think of hundreds and hundreds of miles of unpoliced land. Thousands of Indians there who neither know nor wish to know about your white civilization.

CAMERON:
> The climate's mean and cruel.. Winter comes down like a hammer.

MACGILLIVRAY:
> The natural food of the land, the buffalo, is disappearing fast. The savage people are hungry, and they don't have to be hungry to be nasty.

CAMERON:
> They want no white settlers breaking up the fur trade to build a ten shilling empire in the West. The savages won't stand for it.

LADY SELKIRK:
> Savages, gentlemen. The files of the Hudson's Bay Company show the North West Company could give the savages lessons...

MACGILLIVRAY:
> Lady Selkirk, your understanding of affairs and the sharpness of your tongue are gaining you wide fame. It is the latter, I assure you, more than the former that is carrying your name abroad. Whatever you may read in the Hudson Bay Company papers, my lady, don't confuse civilized justice with the claims and counter claims of trade war...

CAMERON:
> I'll tell you something more, Lady Selkirk, while

we're in your spirited company. The North West
Company wants no colony on the Red River in Indian
territory...

SELKIRK:
Mr. MacGillivray, surely this man is not speaking
for you.

MACGILLIVRAY:
The North West Company doesn't want a native population on the warpath murdering innocent settlers
in an unprotected wilderness. We don't want it.
And we won't have it. There'll be no colonies in
the North West Company's trading territories...

SELKIRK:
Come, come MacGillivray. The North West Company
is an invader and intruder in that territory.
Every document, law and...

CAMERON:
The North West Company, lord silk ears, will pick
up your slummy settlers by the scruff of the...

MACGILLIVRAY:
Now, Now, Cameron, softly...softly. We are, after
all, the guests of a civilized gentleman...

HALKETT:
In the most civilized country in the world.

MACGILLIVRAY:
He is simply trying to tell you, my lord, that you
may not talk of the Indian country as you talk of
London or Edinburgh.

SELKIRK:
Well enough, Mr. MacGillivray, but does that mean
we have to talk of anarchy, chaos, bloodshed and
terror?

MACGILLIVRAY:
Come, come my lord. These are highsounding phrases.

MACGILLIVRAY (cont'd)
> Does Mr. Cameron look to you like the image of the anarchist? Do you believe that we in the North West Company want anarchy and chaos, the very forces to impede quiet and ordered trading in the area? No, no, no. But take a realistic look at the country and the people in it.

CAMERON:
> To tell you frankly, many of the men out there are utterly destitute of moral principle or any of the feelings we associate with civilized society.

MACGILLIVRAY:
> Many are selected because they can deal with the savages on a savage level without too great pain to their consciences. They know why they are in the country...

CAMERON:
> They are there, my lord, to gather furs.

MACGILLIVRAY:
> And they cannot permit too much scruple to come between the intention and the fulfillment of that task.

LADY SELKIRK:
> How well you describe your employees, Mr. MacGillivray. Doubtless, if you run a company staffed with criminals and characterized by terror, that is because the partners, themselves, wish to see terror and savagery used as instruments of policy. The servants of the Company are destitute of moral principle because the Company they work for...

CAMERON:
> <u>Listen</u> to this penny-farthing prating. Come, down <u>on your</u> knees. We'll say a damned Methodist prayer together. (He strikes an attitude of prayer) God save us all from holy meddlers and lordly saints. God save us from...

31

MACGILLIVRAY:
> Come, Come Cameron. Your manners sir. We sail tomorrow...

CAMERON:
> Damn sailing tommorow! Damn manners! Did I come to this house...

MACGILLIVRAY:
> My lord, my Lady Selkirk, we really must be making preparations...

CAMERON:
> ...to go where we'll be free of this damned preaching lord and his damned slanderous wife with a tongue like a cucumber skin.

LADY SELKIRK:
> Your partner, Mr. MacGillivray, tells us much about your operations.

CAMERON:
> Come, MacGillivray, let's leave these gentlefolk to their revels, routs, and rondelays...You may stay for the sermonizing, but I'll be damned if I will.

(Exit Cameron)

MACGILLIVRAY:
> Mr. Cameron likes the ways of the New World. There's a kind of fresh bluntness there. We do really have much to prepare, for we'll be back there soon, at our work. My lord. Mr. Halkett. Remember. It's a good place for gentle people to avoid...Goodbye to you all.

(Exit MacGillivray. Lights out)

Scene Three

(Paul McLoughlin, alone on the stage, in a pool of light)

PAUL MACLOUGHLIN:
Kildonan Settlement, Red River Colony, June 1814. My dearest Elizabeth. Two years parted and still without prospect of you joining me here. Be brave. Things have been unfortunate, but now we seem to move towards better days.

I told you of the slow passage out, the unhappy winter spent at York Factory where the party suffered scurvy, and Governor Macdonnell had to deal with a group of rebels led by George Campbell. Getting here to our destination was a hard and unhappy business. But on September 4, 1813 we held a formal ceremony, launching the settlement. Since that time our numbers have grown slowly, until we number more than 200 souls. We have houses, a mill, sheep, cattle, and good rich land broken and beginning to bear crop. Whatever they tell you about savages, don't believe them. The neighbouring tribes of Indians are all friendly. As a precaution we are armed, of course. And we are happy to show our small field cannon so all will know our strength.

Rumour keeps up about the North West Company - that they intend to smoke us out. They seem to circle and circle about us without striking. At times they are quite generous, and then they turn their backs. We never know. We are becoming a hard target for them. We don't honestly see how they could root us out now, short of open war, and even then the outcome would not necessarily be in their favour. Next year we will have more population. We could well have four or five hundred mouths to feed. And still the Nor'Westers go on stripping the territory of buffalo and shipping out thousands of pounds of pemmican every year. They buy it up and store it away. Governor Macdonnell says they

do it knowing we will run short. He has grown
fearfull of supplies for the settlement. I believe
he is right.

This week he issued a proclamation placing an
embargo on food supplies shipped out of the area.
If this is really Lord Selkirk's territory, then
the North West Company has been poaching for years,
exhausting the resources of the area. Governor
Macdonnell will no longer let them ship pemmican
out. And he has demanded that all hunting from
horseback end. The Metis destroy huge numbers of
the buffalo hunting that way. He says they can
get all they need for themselves by hunting on
foot. The proclamations have not been popular
with anyone but the settlers. There is much
tension in the air, but I don't believe Governor
Macdonnell can do anything else in the circum-
stances...

(Light fade to dark on last sentence)

CAMERON:
> How did you get that letter...?

MACGILLIVRAY:
> As head of this Company it's my business to know how the partners conduct affairs. I'll be asking you, moreover, what hand you played when Miles Macdonnell's people entered Fort La Souris and carried off the pemmican there. But you, John Pritchard, are a damned coward. I know what you did at La Souris. You let those mealy mouthed peasants into the fort to carry off North West Company provisions. You're out, Pritchard. Out. You may retire as peaceably as you like. But out you go.

PRITCHARD:
> I was faced with constituted authority...the writ of the legal governor...I did, under the circumstances...

MACGILLIVRAY:
> Mr. Pritchard. You are taking up the time of the partners of the Company to mewl and puke like a weaning baby. Save it. Save your comments for your diary.

CAMERON:
> The writ of the legal governor...a failed soldier and a ten-shilling empire.

MACGILLIVRAY:
> Don't fear, Pritchard. You won't be stalked. We won't follow you into the bush. We wouldn't waste the manpower. As for your reputation, we'll leave that to the crows; it's garbage.

PRITCHARD:
> (making an exit) Maybe now I'll be able to begin building some reputation...

MACGILLIVRAY:
> I asked you Cameron what hand you had in the

Scene Four
_____

(Fort William. 1814. Lights up on lower stage. A
party comes in vigourously: MacGillivray, Cameron,
Pritchard, MacDonald. A room in the fort)

MACGILLIVRAY:
    (enters talking)...I am sure your foresight, Duncan
    Cameron, is prodigious. I'm sure you study the
    gizzards of crows and cast horoscopes, but you
    haven't done us much good with your back-handed,
    second-guessing wisdom. The Earl of Selkirk is a
    dangerous damned fool. Do-gooders always are. As
    for the governor of the Red River Colony, Miles
    Macdonnell, he's power drunk and mad.

CAMERON:
    You took enough time to stop bowing and begging-
    your-pardon. You liked kissing hands so much there
    in Britain, I expected to see you going around
    behind if we stayed a few days longer.

MACGILLIVRAY:
    Do you think we went to London and Edinburgh to
    take a holiday? To head them, off, to head them
    off.

CAMERON:
    Great strategy. Now there's a colony, proclamations
    - next they'll have a resident bloody army if we
    don't move bloody fast.

MACGILLIVRAY:
    Before you confirm yourself a saint and a prophet,
    Cameron, let me read you a piece of a letter you
    wrote - to the factor at Fort Gibraltar. Just a
    short time ago. "I'd advise you to let Captain
    Miles Macdonnell have some wheat and potatoes on
    his own and his brother's account as I don't look
    on him or his colonists as opponents in trade...
    And should an opportunity offer, you'll no doubt
    give him my compliments..." <u>my compliments</u>.

seizure of the Fort La Souris pemmican. You haven't answered me yet.

CAMERON:
If you'd stop prancing about like King Willy on his goddamned white horse, you might have time to hear someone else's voice than your own. I had no part in that fiasco. If your intelligence lines are working so goddamned well, why didn't you know it?

MACGILLIVRAY:
People who write friendly letters about Miles Macdonnell suggesting cooperation with him may not be understood by all observers. I know very well what you do, Mr. Cameron, very well. You needn't trouble yourself on that head.

CAMERON:
Then you know why I wrote that letter to Fort Gibraltar. The orders were out for begging your pardon and kissing asses, your specialty, and your orders. Maybe you've forgotten with all your running back and forth across the Atlantic and flitting around Montreal like a crown prince. Meanwhile the colony at Red River grows. Buildings go up. And now that lunatic Miles Macdonnell proclaims who shall eat and who shall go hungry.

MACDONALD:
Maybe Mr. MacGillivray intends to buy a share in the Red River Colony and bore from within. Is that why you asked us here?

MACGILLIVRAY:
No, Alexander MacDonald, that madman Macdonnell has laid on the last straw. Did he think he was Holy Martin Luther hammering a notice up on North West Company forts demanding we leave and quit the granted territorites?

MACDONALD:
You said he didn't mean it.

MACGILLIVARY:
>Nor did he. It's a legal way of declaring possession, that's all. He didn't mean it...this year. But the pattern is clear. Either they go or we go. And we're not going anywhere. I suggest we put into action the plan you've been bristling with all these many months.

MACDONALD:
>The sooner the better. The settlers have made fast friends with the Indians. Even the Metis will be harder to stir up than a year ago.

MACGILLIVRAY:
>You'll get that well in hand, Alexander. You've contacts enough in the Indian territory, and an open purse will no doubt help your purpose.

MACDONALD:
>Och, I'll do the job; there's no doubt of that. The Metis will do our bidding. We've trained them well. They know their rights in the interior. Our canny Metis friend, Cuthbert Grant, with his fine Scottish education even believes the Metis people own the land and have more power over it than we do ourselves.

MACGILLIVRAY:
>Good. You'll have a bottomless account to draw on. If you can't seduce the settlers to break up the colony, frighten them. If they won't frighten, buy them...

CAMERON:
>And if they won't buy?

MACGILLIVRAY:
>I think, Mr. Cameron, if they can't be seduced, frightened or bought, some other way of convincing them will occur to you. I don't think for a moment that you lack imagination. They need to learn what happens to anyone who will tamper with our supply lines. For a start I suggest you move among the

settlers, Mr. Cameron, in full regimental costume...

CAMERON:
In full regimental what?

MACGILLIVRAY:
(Opens a trunk and takes out a colourful military jacket) You might put this on for the right effect. Lodge yourself at Fort Gibraltar, with an open hand, and set about the work of winning the settlers from the colony. (MacDonald is helping Cameron put on the jacket)

CAMERON:
In this thing?

MACGILLIVRAY:
You know them there. They love law and order. They love shows of authority and writs and proclamations. A good, rich costume, some braid, and a few medals will have tham all swooning. The loyal and patriotic settlers should be saluting and kissing your arse within a fortnight if you wear the right costume.

CAMERON:
It might work. It just might work.

MACDONALD:
There's more than one way of skinning a cat. We'll have to keep violence out of sight for as long as we can.

MACGILLIVARY:
Violence? I don't remember anybody in this room mentioning violence, Mr. MacDonald. Take care, gentlemen, take care. I have been doing work among the members of the Legislative Councils of Upper and Lower Canada, whatever Mr. Cameron may think about my aristocratic connections. In both Councils they understand the needs of the North West Company. They understand the free and liberal conduct of business and commerce in the New World.

CAMERON:
> Then we set about planning...

MACGILLIVARY:
> With a little help I've brought along. This is a warrant for the arrest of Miles Macdonnell, signed by the Justice of the Peace for the North West, Archibald McLeod...

MACDONALD:
> Arrest? What do we arrest him for?

MACGILLIVARY:
> For breaking and entering, thieving, conspiring, interfering with legitimate business. Oh, there's more, gentlemen, there's more.

MACDONALD:
> Doubtless it's a full and fair setting out of Miles Macdonnell's crimes, since Archibald McLeod is an employee of the North West Company.

MACGILLIVRAY:
> Tush, Mr. MacDonald. Tush. That's a vile insinuation not worthy of a man of your understanding. A justice of the peace always rises above worldly considerations. He doesn't even know who pays his salary. The Sunday School Settlers know more about the honour of the judiciary than you do, thank God.

MACDONALD:
> Do you think Macdonnell is such a fool?

MACGILLIVRAY:
> What does it matter? If he surrenders, we get him out of the way. If he doesn't, we can broadcast him everywhere as refusing to acknowledge the law of the land. Who prates and preaches every time he opens his mouth about the rule of law and civilized order? Macdonnell will be trapped by his own moral cant. We will circle him round with his own legal spells. Then we'll close in.

(Lights out)

Scene Five
_____

(Fort Gibraltar. A scene of revelry. Duncan Cameron in
his military costume. Scene opens with song. Cameron
enters during the singing of it. The song, by T.J.
O'Ray, is sung to the tune of "The Gallant Forty Twa", a
traditional Irish song)

ASSEMBLED CROWD: Take any ten strong farming men
                    Then take a dozen more
                    Add a hungry wolverine
                    To even up the score
                    I'll raise one fist to thrash them all
                    And lay them to their rest
                    They'll rue the day they crossed a man
                    In the pay of the great North West

                    I drink whiskey by the barrel
                    And the earth quakes when I sing
                    I bow my head to no man
                    Be he magistrate or king
                    And when it comes to loving
                    All your ladies know I'm the best
                    You're listening to the boldest rake
                    In the pay of the great North West

CAMERON:
    My friends, my good friends. You're always welcome
to Fort Gibraltar, you're always welcome here.
Though I'm told you're not strongly encouraged to
come here regularly. George Campbell, now, can
any harm be said to come to a settler who visits
here, unless there's harm in good fellowship...

CAMPBELL:
    There's no harm in good fellowship, and there's no
harm in coming to Fort Gibraltar, Captain. Fact
is, it's a place where we've learned a lot. Ay,
and more than songs, too. Here a man can rest a
bit without being told moral lessons and respon-
sibilities.

CAMERON:
    Who'd think of preaching at you that way? And in

North West Company territory.

CAMPBELL:
It's our guardian and keeper, Miles Macdonnell.

CAMERON:
O him. Where is the good fellow tonight?

CAMPBELL:
He's off to Pembina fort to look into more rumours of Indians gathering for attack.

CAMERON:
Well, well. And has good Sheriff Spencer gone with him, do you know?

CAMPBELL:
Not that I know, Captain, but we don't spend a lot of time together since I began visiting Fort Gibraltar.

CAMERON:
Too bad. We've a great and special surprise for Mr. Macdonnell and Sheriff Spencer before the night's through, a surprise we should celebrate. (MacDonald enters, carrying a gun) Ah, MacDonald... any luck?

MACDONALD:
The only action around here's a bit of target practising.

MCLOUGHLIN:
You don't seem to take fear of Indian raids very seriously, any of you.

CAMERON:
Welcome to Fort Gibraltar, Mr...

MCLOUGHLIN:
McLoughlin.

CAMERON:
> Ah yes, McLoughlin. You're a new visitor here. Maybe you were timid about coming while Mr. Macdonnell was in the neighbourhood. No, no, I'm jesting with you about a subject that shouldn't be jested with. To answer your question, yes, we do take savagery in the territories very seriously. That's why I suggest it's time you people closed off the colony and set out for Upper Canada. There's plenty to fear from the Indians.

MCLOUGHLIN:
> There is? We've never seen it. They say they want to be friends. They've even brought us supplies in hungry times.

CAMERON:
> That may well be. There's many willing to call you their friend in order to bring about your destruction. Remember, the Indians and half-breeds think they own the land. They're mad of course. God knows that. But it's enough to give hard steel to these rumours of war.

MCLOUGHLIN:
> Governor Macdonnell says we can protect ourselves against the enemy. But he says it isn't the Indians.

CAMERON:
> Oh no? Who does he say it is?

MCLOUGHLIN:
> The North West Company.

CAMERON:
> Some enemy. Do my offers sound like the offers of an enemy. I guarantee you free and protected journey to the Canadas. (There is something of a scuffle as a man is half admitted, half forces his way into the room)

CAMPBELL:
    Captain Cameron, Sheriff Spencer...

SPENCER:
    I can deliver my own message, man, get out of my
    way (shoving).

CAMERON:
    Sheriff Spencer, you haven't been invited here.
    You're a trespasser. Conduct yourself with more
    propriety sir, or I shall have...

SPENCER:
    Shots have been fired on Fort Douglas and on the
    houses of the settlers in the colony late this
    afternoon, while some of you have been carousing
    at the pleasure of the North West Company.

CAMERON:
    There you are, Mr. McLoughlin, your friendly
    Indians.

SPENCER:
    Indians! A woman from the colony saw everything.
    And she didn't see Indians.

CAMERON:
    Sheriff Spencer, what madness is this?

SPENCER:
    She watched with her husband's glass from behind
    the mill. The shots were fired by men of the North
    West Company.

CAMERON:
    A fine story. And who was the lady to whom you
    refer?

SPENCER:
    I wouldn't tell you her name. Do you think I'm
    mad.

CAMERON:
    As a matter of fact, Sheriff Spencer, yes, I do. Sir, you insult the good name of the North West Company. Is there a man here who believes Nor'Westers would be involved in the kind of savage action this mad man alleges. He was told by a lady hiding behind the grain mill with her husband's spy glass in her hand. What do you suppose the lady was doing behind the grain mill, Sheriff Spencer... and were you there with her yourself, sir?

CAMPBELL:
    Captain Cameron's made us offers more generous than anything we've dreamed of at Lord Selkirk's settlement. Captain Cameron doesn't lock his provisions in vaults when we're hungry, in case one of his important friends might be passing by, in the way of Miles Macdonnell.

SPENCER:
    George Campbell, you are a toady, a hireling, a no-good toadying trouble-maker...

CAMERON:
    Seize that man.

SPENCER:
    Captain Cameron...

CAMERON:
    Hold your tongue, Spencer. You have nothing to say. Hold your tongue and listen to the charges against you. John Spencer, I arrest you in the name of our Royal Sovereign the King, for stealing, sequestering, and removing supplies of the North West Company, to wit, 1400 pounds of pemmican. Likewise I arrest you for forcibly entering North West Company property to seize said goods. I order you to be sent to the City of Montreal to be tried for these charges.

SPENCER:
    By what authority.

CAMERON:
> The warrant is signed, as you will see, by Archibald McLeod, Justice of the Peace for the North West.

SPENCER:
> You mean for the North West Company. What kind of stupid fabrication is this? Let me go! I order you to let me go. (Spencer struggles with his captors)

CAMERON:
> Subdue that man...subdue him. Take him out of here. Put him in irons.

(They exit with Spencer)

MACDONALD:
> There's no call to take insults from any man, Captain Cameron, but you have been a little harsh with Sheriff Spencer, I believe.

MCLOUGHLIN:
> A little harsh is it? I believe it may be you who's mad Captain Cameron. Sheriff Spencer is a good man, whatever orders he may have had to carry out that you disapprove of.

CAMERON:
> Perhaps Mr. McLoughlin. Perhaps in your place I'd feel the same. I respect you, sir. But this man, Spencer, has broken the law.

MCLOUGHLIN:
> Ay, but whose law?

CAMERON:
> John Spencer must go to Montreal for trial. I'd be a criminal myself if I didn't execute the warrant. Though I'm sorry as hell to have to do it.

MCLOUGHLIN:
> You've disguised your feelings well up to this

moment.

CAMERON:
    Mr. McLoughlin, we must all pay due respect to the law of our blessed constitution. It is that which gives us our freedom and dignity as human beings.

MCLOUGHLIN:
    But Sheriff Spencer wasn't stealing anything...

CAMERON:
    Tut, tut, tut, Mr. McLoughlin. The law must be difficult in order to be just. We must submit to it...Indeed, I have a warrant, another warrant, for the arrest of Miles Macdonnell on the same charges.

MCLOUGHLIN:
    With all due respect, sir, I do not believe that you have the right to arrest the Governor of the territory.

CAMERON:
    No, I don't suppose you do think that. But in our system, even the governor of a great territory must submit himself to the laws of the land. Notice how, here, right now, an arrest was made, and there wasn't a shot fired. That is a triumph of law and respect for law.

MCLOUGHLIN:
    I don't like it. I don't like the look of developments here.

CAMERON:
    Neither do I like them, at all. You heard the story about caterwauling savages firing on the colony tonight. How long will it be, do you think, before they launch a full scale attack? I beg you to think of the North West Company's generous offer to relocate you on fine free land in the Canadas. You don't have much time to make a decision. Rumour is running high. Time is running out, Mr. McLoughlin. Time is most definitely running out.
    (Lights down and out quickly)

Scene Six

(Attack on Fort Douglas. 1815. Firing and noise of similar activity just off stage. Could open with someone shot from top level, falling to ground and hastily carried off. George Campbell dashes to join Macdonnell on top level of set)

MACDONNELL:
    Keep your head down, Campbell. If you won't fight, at least don't give us the trouble of hauling your stinking body away.

CAMPBELL:
    There's nobody left to haul it away, Governor Macdonnell. Why don't you see reason...

MACDONNELL:
    O shut up. It's me you're talking to. Three dead. Three. That's all. Three.

CAMPBELL:
    Three dead and three hundred quit.

MACDONNELL:
    Lies again, Cameron's little toady.

CAMPBELL:
    I'm not out shooting settlers, and neither is Cameron.

MACDONNELL:
    No?

CAMPBELL:
    You know he isn't.

MACDONNELL:
    He doesn't need to. He's got his Metis boot licks out there doing it for him.

CAMPBELL:
    Tell that to the settlers. Tell the ones with

houses burned. They don't give a goddamn who used
the torch. They don't care where the bullets are
coming from. They want out while they've got skins
to get out with.

MACDONNELL:
That's Cameron's line. The settlement's strong.
We'll hold.

CAMPBELL:
The Metis have been letting anyone go who wants to
go for good.

MACDONNELL:
Who went?

CAMPBELL:
McKennick, Jamiesons, McLeod, Robertsons, others.
You don't believe me. Then go see for yourself.

MACDONNELL:
You'd watch while I was gone, wouldn't you. You'd
watch the Metis swarm over here while you threw
confetti down on their heads. Save your breath
to cool your porridge, Mr. Campbell. We'll fight
these hired guns until...Who's that coming? Back
there?

MCLOUGHLIN:
Governor Macdonnell.

MACDONNELL:
O, you McLoughlin...Thanks be to the loving lord
and saviour it's you. Keep your head low. They
don't seem near but the bastards can see through a
stone wall.

MCLOUGHLIN:
Campbell? You didn't go.

CAMPBELL:
Not yet.

MACDONNELL:
> He didn't go where McLoughlin?

MCLOUGHLIN:
> Two canoes left today. And not the last to go either, I know.

MACDONNELL:
> Let the parcel of spineless bastards go. The rest of us will hold off these goddamned pow-wows. Eh McLoughlin?

MCLOUGHLIN:
> No. They aren't spineless bastards. They're settlers. They're just people who want to live and grow crops and build. Now they all want to go.

MACDONNELL:
> You too?

MCLOUGHLIN:
> Everybody, pretty well. Why not? We didn't come here to be soldiers. To watch crops burned under our eyes, houses burned. Now they're shooting at us. Killing us. They won't go away ever. We know that now.

MACDONNELL:
> Pull yourself together man. It's a bad time, and it'll pass. They'll go away when we crack the North West Company.

MCLOUGHLIN:
> Who'll be left then? Three dead today. How many by next week, next year? The settlers want to leave, most do.

CAMPBELL:
> All the Metis want is you arrested. It's on your shoulders, all of it.

MACDONNELL:
> Do you know what that means, for the colony?

MCLOUGHLIN:
> I know what it means for the colony if we don't do it.

MACDONNELL:
> You believe that?

CAMPBELL:
> They want you arrested. That's all.

MACDONNELL:
> You believe that McLoughlin?

MCLOUGHLIN:
> Two canoes left, safe.

MACDONNELL:
> They want me to give up?

CAMPBELL:
> They want you to talk.

MACDONNELL:
> Who to?

CAMPBELL:
> They want you to put the white flag up and talk.

MACDONNELL:
> Is that what you want?

MCLOUGHLIN:
> Everyone wants that much...at least.

MACDONNELL:
> Raise up the white flag, then, Mr. Campbell, and see what you can scare up. It's right and proper that you should undertake the task.

(Macdonnell and McLoughlin move to the lower level/front of the fort while he is doing so)

MCLOUGHLIN:
> Will you surrender to them?

MACDONNELL:
>I intend to parley, Mr. McLoughlin. Keep your eye peeled and your gun close at hand. (There is a pause. Then Duncan Cameron appears where they are expecting to greet a half-breed) Well, well, Mr. Cameron, you have taken the task of mediator for lawless marauding half-breeds.

CAMERON:
>No Mr. Macdonnell. I have a warrant for your arrest locked in my desk at Fort Gibraltar, a warrant you have twice refused to acknowledge. Even so, I wouldn't fill the position of negotiator for these savages, acting as they are outside of our blessed constitution.

MACDONNELL:
>Well, then, why are you there, Duncan Cameron, and why not Cuthbert Grant or one of the other Metis leaders?

CAMERON:
>I'd appreciate it, Mr. Macdonnell, if you'd call me Captain Cameron for the sake of form, sir. I'm here for a number of reasons. Not as a negotiator, for that suggests I have an interest in the dispute which you know I don't. I want to end blooshed quickly. Cuthbert Grant and his friends suggested to me that if one of them came forward, they might be shot down under the white flag...

MACDONNELL:
>Mr. Cameron...

CAMERON:
>Captain Cameron, if you please. Your settlers will trust me when I promise safe journey to the Canadas. If Cuthbert Grant had told you that, your settlers might be rightly suspicious.

MACDONNELL:
>Do you...Does Mr. Grant rather, insist upon the

evacuation of all the colonists? Some are determined to give their lives before leaving here.

CAMERON:
No, Mr. Macdonnell. The Metis insist only on your removal for trial. They say you interfered with their trade and livelihood. They see you and Spencer as troublemakers on their lands.

MACDONNELL:
I have been responsible for some woe here. I should have done more to secure the defence of my settlers, that part is true...

CAMERON:
Well, this isn't the place to argue about that, I'm sure. Cuthbert Grant and his friends say you go. Others who want to can remain under the protection of the North West Company.

MACDONNELL:
What choice do I have? For the safety of my settlers, I have to agree to Grant's terms...But the murders have to stop. Tell him that. (Exit Macdonnell)

CAMERON:
(To McLoughlin) Good luck man. A better time's in store for you. (Exit McLoughlin)

MACDONALD:
(Enters and joins Cameron) Well, well, well. That's the last of them.

CAMERON:
It is if Campbell's prediction was right. 140 settlers will set out with Macdonnell to the Canadas, and only 60 will remain behind.

MACDONALD:
A nice piece of work.

CAMERON:
> But it's not finished yet. Gather help. Fire the fort. Fire the mill, fire the stables, fire the barns and grounds. Burn everything Alexander. And take care you don't show a white face at any of the work.
>
> (Lights out)

Scene Seven

(Montreal. Chateau de Ramezay. Winter 1815)

SELKIRK:
    My Lord Sherbrooke, with respect sir, your answers are not good enough. Two years ago your government said the North West Company could keep the peace. Last year you said there was no pressing necessity to patrol the area with forces of order. Now, after a seige, murders, and burning, you speak of tribal battles and trade wars as if they were occurring in the South Seas.

SHERBROOKE:
    You overestimate things. The reports from the Red River are not encouraging, but three people killed, looked at from a strategic angle, is not a lot of life to lose.

LADY SELKIRK:
    If the three were relations of yours, Lord Sherbrooke, you would consider it quite enough.

SHERBROOKE:
    From the human point of view, of course, such troubles aren't easy to bear.

LADY SELKIRK:
    What are the other points of view, besides the human...?

SHERBROOKE:
    (A little ruffled) I refer of course to the trade difficulties, the tribal complications, the budgets we are permitted by the Colonial Office for law and order and military use.

SELKIRK:
    Surely you don't mean British North America cannot afford justice? What of the disbanding regiments of the recent war? It would cost little to maintain them as a force for a few years.

SHERBROOKE:
> They might well upset the balance of power in the area to the detriment of His Majesty's government.

LADY SELKIRK:
> They might?

SHERBROOKE:
> Oh yes, Lady Selkirk, they might bring about a major massing of Indian power in the area.

SELKIRK:
> But the Indians want law and order. There's much testimony to that effect.

SHERBROOKE:
> No they don't Lord Selkirk. They want war. They always want war.

LADY SELKIRK:
> Why would anyone always want war, my lord?

SHERBROOKE:
> You know them, don't you. Warpath and head-hunting and all that. An Indian is only happy with a ring of scalps at his waist and some white woman to rape. It's in their blood. Can't blame the poor chaps all that much, I suppose. It's their country, or was...

LADY SELKIRK:
> Don't you think we should do something to curb those blood-thirsty tendencies?

SHERBROOKE:
> In simple terms, yes, of course. That's the right thing. That's the right thing to do. But things aren't simple. I wouldn't think of shipping a body of men out that way without full clearance from Bathurst in the Colonial Office. I'd have to determine I wasn't upsetting the balance of power in the area. I'd have to consult with the executive bodies of both Canadas...

SELKIRK:
> I see no complications, none. I see the shipment of a hundred regulars to the area. Then we'd have a cheap and easy rule of law.

SHERBROOKE:
> I cannot spare a hundred regulars at this time. Quite impossible.

SELKIRK:
> But they are about to be demobilized some of them right now.

SHERBROOKE:
> That's quite another thing.

LADY SELKIRK:
> Quite another thing?

SHERBROOKE:
> Yes, my lady. I can't afford the money, nor the men.

SELKIRK:
> Put in that way, sir, you throw down a challenge which I'll take up. I will pay for the outfitting of a hundred regulars, of your choice, under officers of your choice, and totally accountable to you in all regards, if you will send them out. I will guarantee their maintenance for two years.

SHERBROOKE:
> That's very generous of you, Lord Selkirk, but it would smack of favouritism and it would alarm people in some quarters.

LADY SELKIRK:
> How so?

SHERBROOKE:
> The Nor'Westers would think I was siding with you. They would think I simply accept one side of the story.

LADY SELKIRK:
> Let's say you accept any side of the story. All sides admit the Colony was razed to the ground, the colonists scattered, three of them killed in gun battle. Do you think you would be taking sides Lord Sherbrooke if you prevented bloodshed, if the peace was secured?

SHERBROOKE:
> Of course I don't Lady Selkirk. You see...

LADY SELKIRK:
> I see that you are afraid to take action to keep the peace in the North West.

SHERBROOKE:
> (Ignoring her remark) Damned vexing problem, Selkirk. But it'll work itself out if we give it time. These things work out, eh? Awfully good of you to ask me here. Splendid to have another gentleman in Montreal. There aren't many I fear. Lots of business men, Selkirk, lot's of that kind. Not many gentlemen, though.

SELKIRK:
> I don't understand the power of the North Westers here. I just don't...

SHERBROOKE:
> Quite frankly, Selkirk, the place takes learning. You haven't learned it yet, that's about what it comes to. Don't take any of that savage-gentle folk business. It don't wash, Selkirk. They're not like us. I'm told they're even built differently, but this isn't the company to go into that.

LADY SELKIRK:
> You haven't listened, Lord Sherbrooke, I begin to feel...

SHERBROOKE:
> Lady Selkirk, it's always a pleasure to spend an hour with you and to hear your sharp wit. Don't

trouble your little head about these men affairs.
Got to go away and cut the ribbon on a new steam
driven vessel. Damned fool things. (Exits)

LADY SELKIRK:
There goes the guiding beacon, the head and front
of a whole new experiment in history.

SELKIRK:
Sherbrooke?

LADY SELKIRK:
Sherbrooke.

SELKIRK:
I don't know if he's a fool or a genius. He's
certainly not evil, but there's more intermarriage
and private dealing in back rooms here than in the
most clannish clan in all the highlands of Scotland.
Speak to one man in this town and you may be speaking to the interests of law enforcement, the fur
trade, provisioners, ship-builders, land companies,
and even John Jacob Astor of the United States.

LADY SELKIRK:
Time, I think, that the Colony was made into an
armed camp. We see what petitions to Sherbrooke
bring. I can't decide if it's worse to get a
letter from him or to talk to him.

SELKIRK:
An armed camp won't solve anything.

LADY SELKIRK:
Let's brandish a few weapons, show some soldiers,
even if our own.

SELKIRK:
In our pay?

LADY SELKIRK:
You suggested it. Sherbrooke will never release
a man for duty in the North West. Meanwhile, you

break against the inactivity and the lies here...
and the destruction of the colony.

SELKIRK:
We can't resort to arms.

LADY SELKIRK:
I didn't say resort to arms.

SELKIRK:
A weapon unsheathed is a weapon ready for use. A weapon brandished invites a response. And that is war. Besides, should I send the peasantry of Europe to the North West as settlers, arm them and have them killed in pitched battle? A noble vision of regeneration.

LADY SELKIRK:
What else can you see then?

SELKIRK:
I see the need to keep pressing Sherbrooke and Bathurst in the Colonial Office. I see the absolute necessity of the rule of law.

LADY SELKIRK:
When I think of those poor folk, and what they've been through, I know the struggle is worth everything. And I'm full of admiration for the man who conceived of the idea and who puts his own needs and pleasures aside to fight for the realization of it. I'm worried for the success of the Colony. I'm worried for your health. I wouldn't want to lose you for all the colonies in North America.

SELKIRK:
Take heart, then. The new shipment of settlers is there. I know of no better men we've ever had than Colin Robertson and the new governor, Robert Semple. If anyone can quiet the emotions of the North West - short of an invading army from the Canadas, it's Robert Semple.

LADY SELKIRK:
> How I hope you're right. I'm getting sick with fatigue and worry. And if I'm sick and sleepless, I know what's happening to you. You must take care, Thomas, for my sake...

HALKETT:
> (His voice is heard off stage shouting) Thomas! Thomas!

SELKIRK:
> I'm here, John. We're in the drawing room.

HALKETT:
> Now I'm here I'm afraid to tell you what's happened. (Sits down) There's been a massacre.

LADY SELKIRK:
> Where?

SELKIRK:
> Not the Red River?

HALKETT:
> Canoes are just in from the West. News running like wildfire in the city. Twenty-one settlers and one Metis dead. That's all we know.

SELKIRK:
> Semple?

HALKETT:
> Killed. Twenty-one settlers murdered. The Metis circled, and when Semple went out to parley, the Metis rode in in waves tightening and tightening the circle till they were firing into the settlers like so many sacks of straw.

SELKIRK:
> Why twenty-one of ours slaughtered and only one of theirs?

HALKETT:
> The settlers went out to parley, almost unarmed, on foot, at dusk. They were sitting ducks.

LADY SELKRIK:
> My God...will it never end?

SELKIRK:
> You were right Jean. You were right, damn it.

LADY SELKIRK:
> It does little good to know that now.

SELKIRK:
> You said make the colony an armed camp.

LADY SELKRIK:
> I did.

SELKIRK:
> It's not too late. I'm going to the colony.

HALKETT:
> With an army?

SELKIRK:
> With an army. And fast.

LADY SELKIRK:
> I didn't mean you to go yourself, Thomas. You're sick. You mustn't go.

SELKIRK:
> (To Halkett) I'll need help with arrangements. We must move fast.

LADY SELKIRK:
> If you go to the Red River Colony, Thomas, I'm going, too. For your sake.

SELKIRK:
> (To Halkett) Can you look into the deMeuron regulars being disbanded? I'll go to the

provisioners...

LADY SELKIRK:
Thomas...

SELKIRK:
Yes my love.

LADY SELKIRK:
I said if you go to the Red River Colony, I'm going with you.

SELKIRK:
I heard you the first time, and you added you're coming along for my sake.

(Selkirk and Halkett exit as lights out)

Scene Eight

(Fort William. 1815. On the watchtower at Fort William)

CAMERON:
    Canoe coming on. With soldiers. Get MacGillivray quick.

MACDONALD:
    MacGillivray! (Runs to exit) Canoe sighted. Soldiers.

MACGILLIVRAY:
    How many?

CAMERON:
    One canoe so far.

MACGILLIVRAY:
    Give me the glass. We are to have a visit from Lord Selkirk I believe.

CAMERON:
    Canoes and more canoes, full of uniforms.

MACGILLIVRAY:
    (Takes the glass again) Well, well, well. The Lord comes with an army...(Moves towards the exit)

CAMERON:
    My glass, MacGillivray. You're taking my glass...

MACGILLIVRAY:
    Oh yes, so I am.

(Blackout. MacGillivray, MacDonald and Cameron enter lower level from under the platform, in a hurry)

MACGILLIVRAY:
    If this is Sherbrooke's doing, we've been double-crossed and there'll be trouble.

MACDONALD:
    Ay, there'll be trouble. Trouble for the North West Company.

MACGILLIVRAY:
    Get rid of these papers.

CAMERON:
    The guards'll hold them up as long as they can. But Selkirk'll be in smartly. They didn't come all this way to stand on formalities at the fort gate.

MACGILLIVRAY:
    Get rid of these papers, and hurry.

CAMERON:
    They've enough force to make a bloody battle if it comes to that.

MACDONALD:
    Surely there'll be no blood where the holy Lord Selkirk is...

MACGILLIVRAY:
    You have your orders. If Lord Selkirk is holy, this is the time to be holier-than-thou. Don't forget.

(Enter Selkirk, Halkett and McNab)

MACGILLIVRAY:
    My Lord Selkirk...gentlemen...welcome to Fort William. This is indeed a surprise and a pleasure. I shall give instructions...

SELKIRK:
    Mr. MacGillivray, among your other vandalisms and depredations, you have prisoner Mr. Pritchard, Mr. Nolin, Pambrun, Bourke, and Macpherson and Hedin, survivors of your Seven Oaks massacre. I presume you are punishing them for managing to have stayed alive.

MACGILLIVRAY:
> You are quick to believe scandal and rumour, Lord Selkirk. Perhaps you would be kind enough to tell me...

SELKIRK:
> Do you deny that you have the men I named here as your prisoners?

MACGILLIVRAY:
> Don't be inflamed my lord, I didn't deny that fact at all...

SELKRIK:
> Are those men in detention, Mr. MacGillivray?

MACGILLIVRAY:
> Passions have been running high, as you must know, and I thought it would be best to keep some men out of harm's way.

SELKIRK:
> We are to believe, I take it, that those you couldn't murder at Seven Oaks, you are starving to death here.

MACGILLIVRAY:
> I should be very very sorry, indeed, to think you could believe that.

SELKIRK:
> Mr. MacGillivray, I order you to release those men at once. (Pause) Sergeant McNab.

MCNAB:
> Suh!

MACGILLIVRAY:
> Mr. MacDonald will you speak to James McLeod below and ask that he give the gentlemen mentioned the freedom of the fort.

SELKIRK:
   Mr. MacDonald...ask Mr. Pritchard to step in right
   away...

MACGILLIVRAY:
   Yes, yes, Mr. MacDonald, pray do as you're bid. Are
   we to take it, Lord Selkirk, that you are conducting
   an armed invasion of this fort?

SELKIRK:
   Sergeant McNab will you please do your duty.

MCNAB:
   Suh! (Places an arm on MacGillivray) William
   MacGillivray, you are under arrest. You are charged
   with being accessory to murder, arson, and you are
   charged with forming a conspiracy to invade the
   lands, buildings and possessions of innocent people
   and to have urged violence against them. You will
   be bound over for good behaviour and taken to
   Montreal for trial.

MACGILLIVRAY:
   I submit to arrest under protest, but I will not
   resist. You will do well to have evidence for the
   charges you have made and no doubt put your signa-
   ture to.

HALKETT:
   (Has opend a box and found a few hastily hidden
   papers) What we don't have as evidence already,
   Mr. MacGillivray - and we have a great deal already
   - will doubtless leap out at us from walls and cup-
   boards hereabouts.

SELKIRK:
   I don't think we need to discuss the status of our
   evidence with Mr. MacGillivray. We will take these
   matters up with the courts.

MACGILLIVRAY:
   Perhaps Lord Selkirk you will explain the presence
   of your army. It would appear you are operating a

private force.

SELKIRK:
Some few of the soldiers travelling with this company are my bodyguards, appointed to assure my personal safety. The rest of the uniformed men are aids to the civil power. They are members of the very recently demobilized deMeuron regiment. They are in my service for a stated period of time after which they will settle in the Red River Colony, which, you will be happy to learn, will shortly be drawn together again.

MACGILLIVRAY:
Lord Selkirk, it is my very strong belief...

SELKIRK:
I am not at this moment interested in your legal commentaries or analyses. We have more important business to conduct.

MACDONALD:
(Enters) Mr. Pritchard will be along shortly.

SELKIRK:
Sergeant McNab, will you continue please.

MCNAB:
Alexander MacDonald. Duncan Cameron...You are under arrest with the same charges against you as William MacGillivray: conspiracy, being accessory to murder and arson, urging violence against innocent people...

MACDONALD:
I had nothing to do with the massacre. MacGillivray and Cameron...

CAMERON:
Lying bastard!..(Flies at him) (Subdued by MacDonald and McNab) (Shakes loose) I'm not going to stay here and listen to these bloody insults. (Makes as if to leave the room)

SELKIRK:
    Seize that man. Carry him away...Sergeant McNab.
    Let as many see Mr. Cameron being tamed as wish to.
    (McNab takes him out subdued)

(Pritchard enters)

MACGILLIVRAY:
    Ah...Mr. Pritchard.

SELKIRK:
    Mr. Pritchard. I have heard much of you sir. And
    I'm pleased after so much time to make your acquaint-
    ance. Especially since you were present at Seven
    Oaks.

PRITCHARD:
    This is an honour, my lord. I was a member of
    MacGillivray's company until I was invited to retire
    early. Then I joined your colony. I was at Seven
    Oaks.

HALKETT:
    Mr. Pritchard, you are rubbing your wrists. Are you
    troubled with rheumatism?

PRITCHARD:
    I was kept in irons.

SELKIRK:
    So that is how you protect harmless subjects who
    come into your care is it, Mr. MacGillivray?

MACGILLIVRAY:
    I don't believe the situation would be improved by
    any comment I could make on it.

SELKIRK:
    Were others kept in irons, too, Mr. Pritchard?

PRITCHARD:
    Yes, some were, but not all. The most brutal treat-
    ment was received by Mr. Bourke. He was kept in

irons though he was wounded badly at the Seven Oaks massacre.

MACGILLIVRAY:
I cannot for the life of me understand how you can call defense against arrogant and senseless attack on innocent Indians and halfbreeds - who then defend themselves with reasonable success - massacre. Where does this word massacre come from anyway? Out of whose steamy imagination does it come?

MCNAB:
(Enters quickly) My lord, we have caught them burning evidence.

SELKIRK:
You stopped them.

MCNAB:
Yes sir.

SELKIRK:
Well get back there man! Record and witness all who were involved. Charge them with obstructing justice...It seems Mr. MacGillivray that for the first time in your criminal career you have been caught and surprised. It seems you have something to hide and evidence to burn...

(Lights out)

Scene Nine

(Fort William. 1815. Just outside the fort. Lady Selkirk and Halkett walking)

LADY SELKIRK:
    Thomas would say that unfair fights are sometimes won, and that makes the winning even better.

HALKETT:
    Nobody but a damned fool looks for an unfair fight to win...He should know that by now.

LADY SELKIRK:
    It makes the odds high, the way it's going...

SELKIRK:
    (Enters) Beautiful evening...Did I hear you mention my name as I came out? Was I the subject of your conversation?

HALKETT:
    You were, Thomas. We were talking about the awful odds we face.

SELKIRK:
    They've had things their way a long time. But we're testing all that now.

HALKETT:
    A lot of good it will do to test, and to lose.

SELKIRK:
    We won't lose. The evidence is hair-raising. Unbelievable. If it turns our stomachs, what do you think it will do in a court in Montreal?

HALKETT:
    I'd have agreed six months ago, but now I'm willing to bet they own enough of the judges in Montreal to get any decision they want.

SELKIRK:
>That kind of statement doesn't become a gentleman. It's the kind of statement, John Halkett, that breeds contempt for the law. If we lose faith in the power of the law and the objectivity of the courts, what remains to us?

HALKETT:
>I've been wondering that for a few days.

SELKIRK:
>There's no other way in civilized society.

HALKETT:
>That isn't strictly true, Thomas. In a situation like this, you move into something like the French Revolution, don't you? You operate force from necessity.

SELKIRK:
>John...

HALKETT:
>You've told me yourself about being at the Bastille and helping with the release of one of the prisoners...

SELKIRK:
>But that was different...

LADY SELKIRK:
>Different than 21 innocent people slaughtered? Different than the burning of the colony? Different than the innocent we found here in irons?

SELKIRK:
>Revolution, as Edmund Burke has written, is the last resort of desperate men. This isn't France. We're not at the point of despair. The courts are there. They work. We'll get a fair hearing and win justice. I'm confident.

LADY SELKIRK:
    We won't win with your tactics, Thomas.
    MacGillivray owns Governor Sherbrooke. He gets to
    Bathurst in the Colonial Office every day. Bathurst
    checks Canada, which means checking with Sherbrooke.
    That's how it happens. A pretty merry-go-round.

SELKIRK:
    John Sherbrooke's an old warhorse. And sick, very
    sick. But I don't believe he intends to do evil.

LADY SELKIRK:
    I don't care whether he intends to or not...he
    succeeds. They're all in it together. Where do you
    think William MacGillivray's house - the richest
    house in North America - comes from? By giving alms
    to the poor? What do you think the lesson of his
    wealth is, his position on the Legislative Council?

HALKETT:
    I know what the lesson is for me.

LADY SELKIRK:
    John?

HALKETT:
    While you two argue the merits of what seems a hope-
    less cause, I have to get back to the evidence.

SELKIRK:
    I'll help you John. I want to go through the
    MacGillivray file.

HALKETT:
    There's work for one. That's all. You'll keep me
    up till dawn with strategies. I'd sooner work alone
    and get some sleep. Pleasant dreams...(Exits)

SELKIRK:
    I'm glad you've come on this trip, Jean. Separa-
    tions become worse each time...

LADY SELKIRK:
 Thomas.

SELKIRK:
 My love?

LADY SELKIRK:
 Thomas, you haven't answered my questions.

SELKIRK:
 Must we go on with that?

LADY SELKIRK:
 You mean you'd rather not?

SELKIRK:
 Well, the whole thing's very complicated, very confused.

LADY SELKIRK:
 Too confused for a poor woman to understand?

SELKIRK:
 No, not that at all.

LADY SELKIRK:
 Well?

SELKIRK:
 The world doesn't go along having right and virtue win every contest, even if we knew for sure what right and virtue are. The world goes along balancing right and wrong most of the time. The job for good people is to try to keep the balance. William MacGillivray's power is only part of it. The forces are a lot bigger than him. If he didn't exist, there'd be another man in his place with the same name.

LADY SELKIRK:
 That's too fatalistic. Someone wins. Someone loses. And for a good reason. It matters to fight hard. I haven't seen much balance in the battle

with the North West Company.

SELKIRK:
Maybe you don't see far enough.

LADY SELKIRK:
...or too far.

SELKIRK:
What do you mean?

LADY SELKIRK:
What do *you* mean?

SELKIRK:
You're about to see the beginning of the end of William MacGillivray and his cohorts.

LADY SELKIRK:
You're wrong. I'm sorry. They'll throw every obstacle in your way. You won't be spared. They'll trump up counter charges. The taking of this fort will be called invasion, an act of tribal warfare, God knows what...God knows what they won't think up...

SELKIRK:
Don't be ridiculous, Jean. I didn't expect this kind of pessimism from you. Wait till you see the evidence. It can't lose.

LADY SELKIRK:
Operate whatever strategy you want, Thomas, but don't play innocent. Tomorrow's taking of evidence is meaningless.

SELKIRK:
Meaningless.

LADY SELKIRK:
Yes. We don't have to hear the evidence tomorrow. Nothing can surprise me.

SELKIRK:
> We aren't holding the examination tomorrow to surprise anyone. We are using a slow and firm method, tried and developed over many years, for achieving justice, for righting wrongs without dissolving society into violence and mayhem. We must honour that system and make it work...

LADY SELKIRK:
> That's a fine speech. It may even be true. But the system of law, order, and the courts in British North America is owned by William MacGillivray and the North West Company.

SELKIRK:
> Don't talk rubbish, Jean.

LADY SELKIRK:
> Rubbish is it? The system is built by people like William MacGillivray. To keep them free from people like you...

SELKIRK:
> What do you suggest we do to remedy the situation? God knows I'd like out of all this...Why don't you give us the benefit of your creative genius? Save us from the channels, so expensive and tedious and time consuming.

LADY SELKIRK:
> All right, Thomas. Go through with the examination tomorrow and as many days as it takes. But deal with William MacGillivray...Don't let him arrive at Montreal for trial...He's the head and shoulders. Decapitate him. Cut the head from the body and the whole Company is thrown into disarray.

SELKIRK:
> Well enough said, but how shall we decapitate William MacGillivray apart from the use of the courts?

LADY SELKIRK:
> Literally...(Pause) Yes. (Pause) It could be done accidentally. He could be given medicine. A canoe could turn over in the rapids.

SELKIRK:
> You could go through with that?

LADY SELKIRK:
> I could go through with it, not because I'd want to, Thomas. Not because I'd like to. The North West Company has taught me we can't win using our methods. I've been counting up the dead, only the dead, to say nothing of the lives ruined and the hearts broken, because of the North West Company. It's in the dozens, Thomas. Who shoulders that responsibility? MacGillivray's life is a little thing to trade for the rest of the lives he will destroy unless he's stopped.

SELKIRK:
> You think we can murder to prevent murder. But our strength has been our honesty, our refusal to use dirty methods - their methods.

LADY SELKIRK:
> Murder's a strong word. Maybe it's the wrong word to use in a trade war.

SELKIRK:
> You think we can murder to prevent murder.

LADY SELKIRK:
> They say it themselves. Sherbrooke says it. Trade wars don't use conventional law. I'm almost convinced the Seven Oaks massacre was an incident in a trade war...You know what that means...

SELKIRK:
> We have the right to remove William MacGillivray.

LADY SELKIRK:
> The responsibility. I no longer believe a single

life is so sacred that you allow dozens of innocent
lives to be taken because you won't raise a hand
against the person causing the murder and mayhem.
The Nor'Westers call it trade war. The Governor
and Council agree. Bathurst plays along. All
right, Thomas, let's have a little justice. Let's
stop them where they least expect it.

SELKIRK:
MacGillivray's death would be enough?

LADY SELKIRK:
I think so.

SELKIRK:
One little death to change the course of history.

LADY SELKIRK:
Yes, Thomas. If you put it that way. (Pause) I'm
thinking of your health, too. I'm wondering how
long you can keep up this pace without your health
breaking down completely. Wearing yourself out,
dissipating your energy, to catch a parcel of
common murderers, thieves, and arsonists...whom
you aren't catching.

SELKIRK:
Sometimes, Jean, I don't think you know me very
well. Sometimes I don't think you know the kind
of man I am. You're suggesting murder, and
rebellion against established authority...

LADY SELKIRK:
You are the established authority in this territory.

SELKIRK:
You're going blind, Jean, blind. We will win.
Patience. Be strong. We'll win by the rule of
law. If we can't win that way, it's not worth
winning.

LADY SELKIRK:
Tell that to the families of the twenty-one people

slaughtered at Seven Oaks, you in your comfortable...

SELKIRK:
> Is that the way to get me? You mean I've got integrity if I murder. Otherwise I'm weak.

LADY SELKIRK:
> Maybe. That may be true. If the terms are bullets and torches and you use petitions and writs, you may be deluded. You may have thrown away all the integrity you think you have.

SELKIRK:
> I can't do it Jean, not if it means my life. They circle round and round. But you break through. If I'm anything, there has to be a civilized way. There has to be justice.

LADY SELKIRK:
> There has to be justice?

SELKIRK:
> Yes.

LADY SELKIRK:
> God, I'm tired. It's late, Thomas. Come to bed. We'll hear enough about justice tomorrow.

ACT II

Scene Ten

(The following examinations are played - or were played in the first production as if being recollected by Selkirk. He is sitting at his desk at one corner of the stage, arranging papers, musing. Lights come up on the raised portion, revealing the examinee who announces himself as if his examination and testimony is running through Selkirk's mind. Then Selkirk picks up with the questioning)

PRITCHARD:
> My name is John Pritchard. I was for a time wintering partner of the North West Company, in charge of the fort at La Souris when Governor Macdonnell entered it and seized pemmican supplies in 1813.

SELKIRK:
> You left the North West Company shortly after?

PRITCHARD:
> I was dismissed, and joined the Red River Colony.

SELKIRK:
> Were you present at the Red River Colony on June 19, 1815?

PRITCHARD:
> I was, yes.

SELKIRK:
> Would you tell us what happened then?

PRITCHARD:
> The story really begins two days earlier on June 17. On that day two Indians of full blood came to visit Governor Semple. They warned him they had seen Alexander MacDonald of the North West Company with a large number of half-breeds on their way to wipe out the colony. The Indians had refused to

support the North West Company. Instead, they had
come to support Governor Semple and the settlers...
We were always friendly with them. We shared in
hard times.

SELKIRK:
What did Governor Semple say?

PRITCHARD:
Governor Semple refused the Indians' aid.

SELKIRK:
Why?

PRITCHARD:
He wished to avoid war. And he believed a gathering of Indian allies might start one. He told the
Indians that he knew white men were causing the
trouble in the area and he refused to make Indians
the victims of white men's policies.
The Indians asked him how he would hold off the
attack if it should come. Governor Semple said he
had been given power by the king. He said he'd
control the Metis by the law he had and by a piece
of paper he would take to them and read. When the
raiders arrived two days later and gathered about
the area beyond the fort, Governor Semple took out
a small party of men. I was one of them.

SELKIRK:
Were you armed?

PRITCHARD:
Some were lightly armed, some unarmed. We went out
to meet the Metis. They stood among some trees on
horseback at a spot called Seven Oaks. As we marched forward, a gun went off in our group. Governor
Semple stopped the movement forward and expressed
great anger. As we came up to the group among the
trees, other raider groups rose up and came from
nearly all directions, circling on horseback. One
of the groups came riding towards us in a long sweep.
As the leader came by he slowed and shouted some-

thing at Governor Semple, calling him a damned
rascal. Governor Semple seized the man's bridle
and the butt of his gun. Someone fired. Riders
came in, whooping and yelling and firing guns.
The first two to be hit were Lieutenant Holte and
Governor Semple himself. The others were shot on
the run or cut down where they stood or sat. More
of the Metis rode in, crescent style. All were
shooting into the huddle of settlers. There was
terrible screaming. Semple's men were helpless.
They tried to hold off the bullets with their hands.

SELKIRK:
    Is that all, Mr. Pritchard.

PRITCHARD:
    The settlers were scalped, torn open with bayonets,
their heads bashed in with gun butts. The raiders
then stripped the mutilated bodies of their clothes.

SELKIRK:
    How did you manage to escape?

PRITCHARD:
    I convinced a halfbreed I knew to take me to a
hiding place. He had me run beside his horse as
he moved out and away from the area of battle
until we came to a place where I could hide and
watch...

(Lights fade to blackout on the upper stage. Selkirk
busies at his desk)

(Lights come up on upper platform to reveal Alexander
MacDonald, manacles on his hands)

MACDONALD:
    My name is Alexander MacDonald.

SELKIRK:
    Your position?

MACDONALD:
> Wintering partner with the North West Company.

SELKIRK:
> Mr. MacDonald, do you know anything of the gifts to be given to certain halfbreeds?

MACDONALD:
> Yes, I do. The time has come to speak out, to undo the bad things.

SELKIRK:
> What do you know about the gifts given and the list of halfbreeds to be rewarded?

MACDONALD:
> I know people did things they shouldn't. You've got to understand. They said we had to...Nobody meant any harm...

SELKIRK:
> Mr. MacDonald, did you hear my question?

MACDONALD:
> Which question, my lord?

SELKIRK:
> What do you know about the gifts given and the list of halfbreeds to be rewarded?

MACDONALD:
> They were to be paid.

SELKIRK:
> What for?

MACDONALD:
> For work they did, for work they were told they should do.

SELKIRK:
> What work, Mr. MacDonald?

MACDONALD:
    The pacification of the Red River Colony.

SELKIRK:
    Do you mean the events at Seven Oaks?

MACDONALD:
    Some things went too far...I don't think people intended...

SELKIRK:
    People?

MACDONALD:
    The partners.

SELKIRK:
    Intended what?

MACDONALD:
    To have the bodies cut up and stripped and robbed.

SELKIRK:
    What did they intend?

MACDONALD:
    I've already told you!

SELKIRK:
    Did you help plan the raid on the Red River Colony? (Pause) Did you?

MACDONALD:
    Yes.

SELKIRK:
    Did you help steal the furs from Fort Qu'Appele and re-mark them?

MACDONALD:
    Yes.

SELKIRK:
Why?

MACDONALD:
The partners decided it.

SELKIRK:
Mr. MacDonald, you signed a paper. In it you say that a policy was agreed to at a meeting here, at which you, Duncan Cameron and William MacGillivray were present. You say that policy was to destroy the Red River Settlement by bribery, coercion, or any other means necessary.

MACDONALD:
Yes, my lord.

SELKIRK:
Have you anything to add to it?

MACDONALD:
Only that some of us didn't like what was going on, but we didn't have power to stop it. It would be a sad mistake and a miscarriage of justice if we were punished for things we couldn't prevent.

SELKIRK:
That will be all, Mr. MacDonald.

(Lights on the upper stage go down and out. They come up on William MacGillivray)

MACGILLIVRAY:
My name is William MacGillivray. I am the governor of the North West Company and I am in command of this fort or any North West Company fort when I am present.

SELKIRK:
You are aware of the attacks and the deaths at the Red River Colony.

MACGILLIVRAY:
> I am as aware as anyone else is who has heard of the attacks.

SELKIRK:
> You know the evidence against your partner, Alexander MacDonald?

MACGILLIVRAY:
> I have heard rumours. I know of no convincing evidence.

SELKIRK:
> Mr. MacGillivray, are you standing before this examination absolving Alexander MacDonald?

MACGILLIVRAY:
> I am certainly not doing that because I don't have the information to absolve him or to accuse him.

SELKIRK:
> Did you have any knowledge of his role in the massacre at Seven Oaks?

MACGILLIVRAY:
> I only know, as I have known for some time, that the people in charge of the Red River Colony were offending the Indian and halfbreed people, provoking them, and causing tensions that might break out into warfare. The halfbreeds would never have accepted Macdonnell's order that they mustn't hunt buffalo from horseback. And then, of course, when Governor Semple fell on a troop of them, they could do nothing but defend themselves.

SELKIRK:
> The North West Company employs Mr. Cuthbert Grant, does it not?

MACGILLIVRAY:
> It does.

SELKIRK:
> Do you feel at ease paying Mr. Grant a salary knowing that he robbed furs from Mr. Pambrun and brought them here to be re-marked on Mr. MacDonald's orders? And that he led the attack that resulted in 21 deaths at Seven Oaks?

MACGILLIVRAY:
> I would suggest that the question is asked badly, boldly, and without full reference to possible context of activity. Yes...the question requires latitude, circumstantial interpretation, and a careful definition of the words used in relation to the context given. Furs taken, or held, at the time of a trade war, may be variously described as being held, robbed, confiscated, or frozen - placed in escrow, as it were, or placed in trust, as you allege you have placed this fort in trust until the arbitration of Governor Sherbrooke can be sought to settle different claims upon it.

SELKIRK:
> No, Mr. MacGillivray, until action can be taken against murderers, arsonists, plunderers and thieves.

MACGILLIVRAY:
> I cannot argue with you about definitions, my lord. I don't intend to waste either of our time doing so.

SELKIRK:
> Do you not realize that governors Macdonnell and Semple were the highest powers in the Red River territory?

MACGILLIVRAY:
> Did you expect us to stand idly by, to effect no retaliation for incursions upon our property and interests...

SELKIRK:
> You are advocating, I take it, the use of warfare and not the use of the civilized processes when the North West Company feels itself aggrieved?

MACGILLIVRAY:
> My lord, the civilized processes have not yet been
> firmly established in the North West. I uphold
> the ideal of law and order probably more passion-
> ately than you do yourself. But in the North West
> the man who waits for court justice often waits
> longer than any of the half-civilized people in
> the area will bear.
> The whole silly affair has simply got to be seen
> in proper context, and it disappears like the air
> from a balloon. Much too much is being made of
> events. A trade war, alas, has broken out for a
> short time. One seizure has brought on another
> until the late unfortunate affair of Mr. Semple
> and his people who by an extraordinary infatuation
> went out to attack the halfbreeds...

SELKIRK:
> An extraordinary infatuation...

MACGILLIVRAY:
> Just so, my lord, an extraordinary infatuation, on
> the same level I would judge, as the emotion that
> brought you to seize this fort, the private prop-
> erty of the North West Company. And, moreover,
> for what mad reason I cannot say, the emotion that
> has had you negotiating, buying and signing owner-
> ship papers for everything but the palisades of
> this fort, and all this from the least responsible,
> most drunken partner the Company maintains.

SELKIRK:
> I have my reasons, Mr. MacGillivray. And Mr.
> MacDonald to whom you refer, has sworn most serious
> allegations against yourself and the Company...

MACGILLIVRAY:
> He will unswear them, never worry. What kind of
> piracy is it that permits the crippling of reason-
> able trade then?

SELKIRK:
> Your so-called reasonable trade has caused the

murder of 21 people at a go, pain and heartbreak to many more. I consider all North West Company employees in the Red River territory as rebels, acting maliciously against His Majesty's peaceful subjects. I do not intend to permit the passage of supplies and weapons to rebels in arms.

MACGILLIVRAY:
I want it recorded that I consider this wanton and needlessly punitive act against the North West Company an act of piracy, of lawless, vindictive interference with free and liberal trading rights.

SELKIRK:
Your objection will be noted.

(Lights down and out on upper stage. Halkett enters to Selkirk seated at his desk)

HALKETT:
A letter from Governor Sherbrooke, at last. (He puts the letter in Selkirk's hand. Selkirk reads it) Well...?

SELKIRK:
Both good and bad.

HALKETT:
How so?

SELKIRK:
Commissioners have been named to look into the dispute, to examine the evidence I've collected, and to report to the Governor in Council. But I'm no longer in charge. All legal power in the North West is placed in the hands of the Commissioners until further notice. Chief Commissioner is William Bachelor Coltman, lawyer and member of the executive council of Lower Canada...

HALKETT:
Of which William MacGillivray is a member.

SELKIRK:
>...and the second Commissioner is Mr. John Fletcher, a police magistrate...

HALKETT:
>...and an unreformed drunk. What are we to make of it?

SELKIRK:
>Do you really wonder, John?

HALKETT:
>I do indeed.

SELKIRK:
>It's what we've been waiting for. The evidence is heaped up. I've warrants out for the arrest of the halfbreeds on charge of murder. Poor devils are only the instrument of MacGillivray and Cameron and MacDonald. The charges against those three as accessories looks very very convincing. Even prejudiced observers will have to shift position when they see what we have managed to put together.

HALKETT:
>You have confidence in the Commission?

SELKIRK:
>I have been asking for it for months.

HALKETT:
>They'll do the right thing, you think.

SELKIRK:
>I'm confident. Now we move. Now things go ahead.

HALKETT:
>Thomas, Thomas. What's a Royal Commission? Government pay-off to slow down action, disperse real evidence. Buy time. Buy loyalty. Do nothing.

SELKIRK:
> More aphorisms, John. Witty, but not very close to reality.

HALKETT:
> So now we get them. We have them surrounded. The Commissioners go in for the kill.

SELKIRK:
> If you like.

HALKETT:
> You speak as if your own slate were unblemished.

SELKIRK:
> Well?

HALKETT:
> For them it certainly isn't. You took the fort to secure the peace. You stopped provisioning of Western points for the same reason. But your buying everything not fastened to the ground here, and from MacDonald, a man the partners now obviously despise, is an indiscretion, Thomas, which they will make much of.

SELKIRK:
> If the colonists are to survive, the North West Company must be broken.

HALKETT:
> You think that will help destroy the Company?

SELKIRK:
> I know it will.

HALKETT:
> I thought you wanted to break MacGillivray by legal means, by civil process.

SELKIRK:
> I've purchased everything here by legal means, with Mr. MacDonald co-operating. Signed and witnessed. What's more...

HALKETT:
>The man's your prisoner...hardly conventional. Can you convince a court you aren't coercing him?

SELKIRK:
>They'll be convinced. They will inspect the evidence here and report back to Sherbrooke. The moment we've waited for has come at last. We have nothing more to do now, at the present, but provide a summary of all the evidence, ship off the final batch of men charged, leave a guard here to hand the fort over to Commissioner Coltman and go to Red River and prepare for the arrival of the blessed fact-finders there. The tide begins to run our way, John. The game's ours now.

(Lights out)

Scene Eleven

(Montreal/London. 1816)

(In the first production this scene was called the rondelay. Bathurst occupies the top level. Sherbrooke is seated at his desk on the second level. And MacGillivray moves from the lowest level up and down as he wishes to move closer to or farther from Sherbrooke. Lighting is employed to focus on and off Sherbrooke and Bathurst, giving a sense of distance and of time passing)

MACGILLIVRAY:
> (Who is in conversation with Sherbrooke) When may we expect some justice, Lord Sherbrooke?

SHERBROOKE:
> I understand your impatience, Mr. MacGillivray. It is taking Commissioner Coltman a devil of a time to get reports in. But he is making some headway. It's very complicated. Not an easy matter.

MACGILLIVRAY:
> The charges against me...

SHERBROOKE:
> Most embarrassing...But we mustn't consult together about them, of course...you and me. Wouldn't be proper. Look now. I must communicate with Bathurst at the Colonial Office and get advice.

MACGILLIVRAY:
> You could give orders, yourself, to speed things. Your way should be open...

SHERBROOKE:
> Should be, could be, might be, but isn't. Unlike others, I must seem to be doing justice at all times. You see the difficulty of that.

MACGILLIVRAY:
> A firm action against the marauding settlers would

gain the approval of all reasonable men.

SHERBROOKE:
I've no doubt...if we could find any. There's another side. It isn't only Lady Selkirk who says to me that I should count up the dead settlers and colonists, and then try to find anyone killed by the Red River people.

MACGILLIVRAY:
Alexander MacDonald makes her case hard to believe.

SHERBROOKE:
Damned hard.

MACGILLIVRAY:
Charge follows counter charge. You must want action.

SHERBROOKE:
Oh, yes, by all means, action. We must have action soon, at all costs.

MACGILLIVRAY:
In short, the settlers have to be dealt with.

SHERBROOKE:
Something definitely has to be done.

MACGILLIVRAY:
You are then, I take it, for some firm action... (pause to let Sherbrooke begin response)

SHERBROOKE:
Certainly....

MACGILLIVRAY:
...against marauding settlers. (Before Sherbrooke can come back) First, then, as a firm beginning, Bathurst must be apprised of all the contradictions and complications. He must see matters with crystal clarity, if he is going to permit you to act. (Sherbrooke is going to speak. MacGillivray

holds his hand out as to say "stop" and goes on)
On that very question of the testimony of Alexander
MacDonald, you would have to say something like: (He
begins to speak as if he is dictating a report) The
testimony of Alexander MacDonald, my lord, taken at
Fort William, sworn, witnessed and recorded, was
taken while the said MacDonald was, in fact, a
prisoner of war.

SHERBROOKE:
(Picks up a paper and reads on, exactly where
MacGillivray has left off) The said testimony, many,
many, pages thick was sent on to me. No sooner, however, did MacDonald get away from the fort and from
Selkirk's power, than he unswore the whole, and now
swears he was tortured, made drunk (which I'm told
isn't difficult with MacDonald), and was forced to
sign a statement against his will. My lord, I feel
I must underscore a very important part of that case.
You will remember...

(Lights come up on Bathurst reading exactly where
Sherbrooke leaves off. Lights down on Sherbrooke)

BATHURST:
...that Alexander MacDonald is also the former North
West Company partner from whom Lord Selkirk bought
every last movable material and good from Fort
William, and did do while the said MacDonald was his
prisoner. (Bathurst sits down and begins to write.)
My dear Sherbrooke. I cannot disguise my concern
and even consternation when I read your account of
the kind of testimony taken by the court of information struck by Lord Selkirk. Damn the man,
Sherbrooke, we've had nothing but trouble since he
began his hare-brained scheme of colonization. I
know you think you've had a bumpy road and want to
get out. Have a little patience. I'm looking
around. I may be able to satisfy you when we get
this business straight. The Colonial Office has
stayed out of these matters, these difficulties, as
you well know, Lord Sherbrooke. Do you think a
point on the map in British North America is all we

have to worry about? Regulate yourselves, gentlemen...(Light fades out. Comes up on Sherbrooke)

SHERBROOKE:
(Laying down the letter and turning to MacGillivray) ...regulate yourself, Mr. MacGillivray. I gave you specific information to carry to your partners that they were to do no violence under any conditions, to subjects of His Majesty.

MACGILLIVRAY:
We have done none, I swear it to you, my lord. I gave myself to an arrest warrant - foolish as it was - without turning a hair, in my own headquarters fort. Lord Selkirk has turned away three warrants for his arrest. And he has locked up the undersheriff for the Western District for presuming to bother him with a warrant. The damned settlers are destroying trade, hampering commerce, claiming the land as theirs...

SHERBROOKE:
(Reading from a letter to Bathurst, or writing) ...claiming the future as theirs. Selkirk and his settlers are equating profitable trade with oppression and criminality. I fear Lord Selkirk is mad - possessed by some insane dream. Damn the man. We've had nothing but trouble since the harebrained scheme of colonization. Then...(light fades)

BATHURST:
(Light comes up on Bathurst)...he resists, refuses to submit to a warrant for his arrest. (Bathurst puts down the letter. Begins a letter himself) My dear Sherbrooke. Perhaps a little distance might be of advantage to your view just now. Your reports show unnatural heat on these matters recently...I guess the Highland chief isn't quite as easy to handle as an Indian chief, eh Sherbrooke. (He chuckles)

SHERBROOKE:
> (Lights down on Bathurst, up on Sherbrooke) (Turning from the letter) Eh, Mr. MacGillivray (Picks up the chuckle and repeats it. MacGillivray picks up Sherbrooke's chuckle, twists it) But I still must push everything back on you. Sorry old chap. But there's a lot of territory out there. Spread yourselves around in it. Regulate yourselves. We don't want to interfere. It isn't policy. If you force us to do so, the big timber may burn with the brush, as I'm told you chaps say out there.

MACGILLIVRAY:
> But we can't spread ourselves out. Why do you think we've come here?

SHERBROOKE:
> Nonsense, Mr. MacGillivray. British North America is a large place.

MACGILLIVRAY:
> My lord doesn't seem to understand. Selkirk occupied Fort William. He has stopped supplies going West. He has called the North West Company ...(Lights down on MacGillivray if he is standing far enough off from Sherbrooke)

SHERBROOKE:
> (reading)...rebels in arms against the King's subjects. He charges everyone in sight with crimes, and he holds - and may be sacking at this moment for all we know - four North West Company forts where he has frozen all shipments of furs and trade goods. (Lights down, and up on Bathurst, speaking out into space)

BATHURST:
> Surely all this will blow over, given a little time. Maybe if the Indians could be persuaded to leave the damn colony alone...

BATHURST AND SHERBROOKE TOGETHER:
> You people...(Lights down on Bathurst)

SHERBROOKE:
    ...always misjudged Selkirk, right from the start.

MACGILLIVRAY:
    Selkirk is mad. He wants to destroy the North West Company. Even if he fails, there'll be starvation in the West and no regular shipment of furs to London and Montreal. Trade and commerce are frozen.

SHERBROOKE:
    (Writing) Trade and commerce are frozen. No orders can be made on London merchants.

BATHURST:
    (Here the action speeds up. Bathurst speaks into space. MacGillivray answers directly, to the dumb surprise of Sherbrooke) There will be no shipment of furs from Montreal?

MACGILLIVRAY:
    No, my lord.

BATHURST:
    When do the yearly orders go out to the London merchants:

MACGILLIVRAY:
    They go out regularly on a date that fell exactly three weeks ago.

BATHURST:
    How large was the order this year?

MACGILLIVRAY:
    There has been no order this year. The merchants in the Canadas are talking to U.S. suppliers. The traders are going round us now, talking to buyers in the U.S. fur market. Merchants and traders here are saying much.

BATHURST:
    I'm afraid I've heard a great deal from them myself.

BATHURST cont'd:
As if I regulate...Damn Lord Selkirk. Damn him. And damn the North West Company. Trade is about to stop. (He now speaks a little as if at a public meeting) British commerce is being frozen. British interests are threatened. British business is being scuttled right back to the City of London. All to please a damned idealistic Scottish chieftain. (Sits down to write) My dear Sherbrooke. You need trouble your head no longer about rights and wrongs in the matter. We have taken all the advice possible and we have thought out all the eventualities. You will, therefore, without delay, take care that an indictment be preferred against Lord Selkirk... and you will take the necessary and usual measures in such cases for arresting his Lorship and bringing him before the court from which the process is issued.

SHERBROOKE:
(Reading with MacGillivray looking over his shoulder) I remain, sir, yours, etcetera, etcetera, Lord Bathurst. Well, there you are MacGillivray... (Sherbrooke waves the letter a little. MacGillivray exits) This is a rum business Bathurst.

BATHURST:
(Light stays up on Sherbrooke. Both relax) A Scot, Sherbrooke, is bad enough at the best of times. A Scot with morals is a freak of nature. A Scottish lord with morals is a cross between an Irish saint and a pirate. I prefer one or the other.

SHERBROOKE:
Whatever they say about Selkirk, he's a gentleman. I've never seen any different.

BATHURST:
I suppose you've heard he comes up for election again this year.

SHERBROOKE:
House of Lords is it.

BATHURST:
>   You know the system for getting a few Scotties in
>   without swamping the place...They're all lords in
>   Scotland, if you listen to them.

SHERBROOKE:
>   He's in the House now, I know. He's told me.

BATHURST:
>   He's out this time, unless he gets some strong
>   bodies behind him.

SHERBROOKE:
>   Well?

BATHURST:
>   Tell him Sherbrooke, that if he'll come back to
>   prepare for the election, I'll guarantee his place.

SHERBROOKE:
>   If not?

BATHURST:
>   Shrug your shoulders, Sherbrooke. Look enigmatic.
>   Dragging poor Lady Selkirk across the Atlantic
>   when he didn't have to.

SHERBROOKE:
>   She believes it all, every bit, as if it were her
>   own idea. She nearly converts me every time I see
>   her. Had a baby girl recently...a fine baby, and a
>   fine woman that one. My wife's the godmother and
>   the child has her name.

BATHURST:
>   Not like real fighting action, is it? Bloody
>   wearing business. But I'm getting you out of it
>   soon. Keep pushing him to come back if you can. I
>   could still get him that place in the Lords if
>   he'll come over. The whole damned thing's a shame.

SHERBROOKE:
>   I don't know what anyone would want to do here. I

>   don't like it. I can follow orders, but nothing's
>   clear. I know I seem confused, but it's the place.

BATHURST:
> It's the place, Sherbrooke. I remember the Duke of
> Wellington describing you as the most passionate
> man he had ever known.

SHERBROOKE:
> But I was younger then...

BATHURST:
> Ay, and so was he...

(Lights down and out)

Scene Twelve

(Trials in the Canadas. 1817)

JUDGE:
    How do you plead?

SELKIRK:
    Not guilty.

JOHN BEVERLEY ROBINSON:
    My lord, the prosecution is anxious to proceed with the case as speedily as possible, especially since Lord Selkirk protested loudly at having to travel here.

JUDGE:
    Well then, let us proceed.

ROBINSON:
    I'm afraid Lord Selkirk has objections, my lord.

JUDGE:
    Oh...objections, _again_, Lord Selkirk.

SELKIRK:
    I should think you would know them by now. My lawyers have already made strong objections directly to Lord Sherbrooke on this charge.

JUDGE:
    Lord Sherbrooke does not preside over this court, Lord Selkirk, I do.

ROBINSON:
    Lord Selkirk will try almost any device to make court proceedings swing into his pocket.

SELKIRK:
    I have written the same things to both the prosecution and to this court.

JUDGE:
> Thank you Lord Selkirk. I cannot, of course, receive private pleadings from parties charged with crimes. Everything must proceed in open public tribunal. If you wrote, you did not appeal to be heard by judge in chambers.

SELKIRK:
> My objections to the proceedings...

JUDGE:
> (Interrupts) You may now tell the court your objections to the proceedings.

SELKIRK:
> The charges are for resisting arrest and for jailing the undersheriff who pursued me and attempted to have me seized.

JUDGE:
> He describes the charges correctly, Mr. Robinson?

ROBINSON:
> Yes, my lord.

JUDGE:
> Well, Lord Selkirk?

SELKIRK:
> The governor had lifted, by Proclamation two months earlier, anyone's right to make arrests or lay charges in the North West except Commissioner Coltman. This court, therefore, has no jurisdiction. I cannot resist an arrest that is against the law to make.

ROBINSON:
> But Lord Selkirk imprisoned the undersheriff.

SELKIRK:
> To stop him harassing me. To stop him from trying to carry me off in a kidnap.

JUDGE:
> That is the substance of your objection, Lord Selkirk?

SELKIRK:
> It is. And it's irrefutable.

JUDGE:
> Lord Selkirk, this court will decide what is refutable and what is irrefutable. Thank you.

SELKIRK:
> What does the court decide?

ROBINSON:
> Perhaps you would like time, my lord, to study the arguments. It may well be that in a case of criminal activity a sheriff's right to arrest would exceed the powers of a Proclamation. I certainly require a remand. I need some time to look into the precedents for such an objection.

JUDGE:
> Would two weeks give you time enough, Mr. Robinson?

SELKIRK:
> Two weeks...the issue is crystal clear.

JUDGE:
> Please...Lord Selkirk...

ROBINSON:
> With respect, my lord, I'd be happier with three weeks.

JUDGE:
> Can you be present in three weeks, Lord Selkirk?

SELKIRK:
> I must travel two hundred miles, my lord. The matter might be looked into in the next few days. The precedents cannot be that complex.

JUDGE:
> We could make a hasty judgment, Lord Selkirk, and prevent you from facing a little physical discomfort. But that is irrelevant. Should we decide justice by the distance a person has to travel to court? Hardly. Three weeks from today, then. In this court. I will give my findings on the objection, and the arguments of the prosecution. You may both, in the meantime, present your arguments in writing. The case is recessed for three weeks.

(Lights down and out)

Scene Thirteen

(Montreal. 1818)

HALKETT:
 Day by day and hour by hour the situation gets worse. They've let Cuthbert Grant out on phony bail, with two charges of murder against him.

LADY SELKIRK:
 No one lifts a hand. Archie MacLennan, too.

HALKETT:
 Charged with murder and permitted to flee the coop.

LADY SELKIRK:
 You pay 6000 pounds bail. They pay a few pounds and are allowed to slip away. We're losing Thomas.

SELKIRK:
 Losing? This is mayhem. They free murderers, self-confessed murderers, to run away. That's not losing. It's mayhem.

LADY SELKIRK:
 Wake up, Thomas. It's losing. And it's mayhem. It's policy and strategy. Miles Macdonnell has been bumped from court to court for three years, the whole time denied a judgment for or against him. That's planned psychological violence. You just don't want to believe it.

HALKETT:
 Don't you see yet?

SELKIRK:
 Maybe you don't get justice in every small case. But you work to fashion a just system. If not, what's the alternative? Would you prefer the absolute injustice of the MacGillivray's. Swift, sure, and unfumbling?

LADY SELKIRK:
> What happens to Governor Semple and the settlers in the meantime? Where's justice for them?

SELKIRK:
> You hang corpses around my neck. Did I murder them?

LADY SELKIRK:
> Well, Thomas...?

SELKIRK:
> I know the argument. Good men should shoot first. But they can't. They have to fight and fight, and maybe lose a lot, to make a system that ends the shooting for good. I often want to shoot first, but deep inside me, I know I'd be wrong...there's a better way. (As he speaks the last lines, Miles Macdonnell comes in and announces his presence with a cough)

LADY SELKIRK:
> Ah, Mr. Macdonnell, you've come to see us. Perhaps among all this soiled conversation you bring some cheery news.

MACDONNELL:
> Some may think so, but not me I fear.

LADY SELKIRK:
> But you have news.

MACDONNELL:
> Sir John Sherbrooke is to be replaced.

HALKETT:
> Doubtless by Lord Dalhousie who's been waiting in the wings of Nova Scotia to hear the sad and cheerful news these many months.

MACDONNELL:
> Wrong. We are to have a Duke as Governor General, the Duke of Richmond, who, in case you are not familiar with the peerage, is the brother-in-law

of Lord Bathurst. And in case you don't know the
economics of the peerage, the Duke of Richmond is
in such a bad state of financial ruin that even
a position in Canada has to appeal to him. So he
comes here.

HALKETT:
Do you think Richmond will be better?

SELKIRK:
No. The class in power does nothing but line its
own pockets just now. I can't believe that gentlemen - members of my own class - could act with
such cynicism. Lord Bathurst acts only to secure
British commercial interests. The lives of British
subjects don't mean a thing to him - let alone the
lives of Indians or halfbreeds. John Sherbrooke...
well, he fumbled. But he knew he couldn't betray
his class. He never once betrayed his class.

HALKETT:
And the mark upon you, Thomas, is the mark of the
betrayer of his class.

SELKIRK:
Thomas Douglas, fifth Earl of Selkirk, Scottish
member of the British House of Lords, betrayer of
my class? Helper of the dispossessed of Great
Britain and Europe. Securer of the loyalty of
British North America. Holder off of the terri-
torial ambitions of the United States. Builder
here of a territory of free, justly-ruled, self-
respecting souls...betrayer of my class.

HALKETT:
Cheer up, Thomas. Maybe the garden by the Red
River will be tilled to feed the world someday.

SELKRIK:
Greed, I'm afraid, has no community.

HALKETT:
And the men of your class can't see beyond the fur

trade and their present profit ledgers.

SELKIRK:
> Meanwhile cases pile up in the courts. Our associates are charged and need help. The settlers must be defended with every energy we have. Come along. Others may theorize. We have to work.

LADY SELKIRK:
> Couldn't you forsake them for a little while, for some rest?

SELKIRK:
> Rest? Rest? Oh yes...If I try to sleep I lie and hear the watch calling each hour. The evil of the whole thing gnaws at me. Innocent men driven to near madness by a government that uses them like puppets. Every hour I stay awake, at least I can say that I've spent another hour trying to get justice for those poor, defenceless bodies...

LADY SELKIRK:
> Poor, defenceless bodies...?

SELKIRK:
> Do you doubt that?

LADY SELKIRK:
> Not a bit, Thomas.

SELKIRK:
> What did you mean then?

LADY SELKIRK:
> You begin to look a poor defenceless body yourself. You can't be at all the settlers' trials.

MACDONNELL:
> You can't be at all your own trials; Sandwich, York, Quebec, Montreal.

LADY SELKIRK:
> Tomorrow what is it?

SELKIRK:
    Sandwich.

LADY SELKIRK:
    Next week?

SELKIRK:
    York.

LADY SELKIRK:
    After that?

SELKIRK:
    Sandwich again.

LADY SELKIRK:
    Round and round.

HALKETT:
    Round and round.

SELKIRK:
    Round and round.

(Lights out)

Scene Fourteen

(1818. Trial. Upper Canada)

SELKRIK:
    My lord, before we begin this hearing I object to the fact that two members of the jury are employees of the North West Company. Mr. Stevens and his brother are by definition interested parties in this case.

CHIEF JUSTICE POWELL:
    That is a nice point you raise, Lord Selkirk, and I thank you for drawing the court's attention to it. But both men are reputable subjects and both of them are under oath, as you know. I have no doubt if they believed their own interests were involved in the trial they would make the fact evident to me. They have not done so...I must overrule your objection...will you proceed, Attorney-General Robinson?

ROBINSON:
    My lord, I have examined, with advice, the charge against Lord Selkirk for false imprisonment of undersheriff Smith, and I find that to my surprise there is an irregularity.

POWELL:
    Yes Mr. Robinson.

ROBINSON:
    The Proclamation of Lieutenant Governor Gore lifting all magisterial powers previous to the actions of the Royal Commission did indeed make the warrants for Lord Selkirk's arrest invalid.

POWELL:
    I see, Mr. Robinson, and what do you intend to do?

ROBINSON:
    I intend to drop the charge, my lord, and proceed with another.

POWELL:
   Quite, Mr. Robinson...

SELKIRK:
   My lord...

ROBINSON:
   Yes, my lord, I wish to proceed with a charge against Lord Selkirk for conspiracy to injure or destroy the trade of the North West Company, by undertaking various acts of injustice and oppression in August and September and October of 1816 so as to conspire, collude and combine to do damage to the good name and to the physical property and possessions and to the free trade and commerce of said Company...

SELKIRK:
   Objection, my lord.

POWELL:
   Lord Selkirk.

SELKIRK:
   I have had no notice of this charge. I have only a witness or two present, by accident, to call on the matter. We have had no time to consult and prepare our case.

POWELL:
   Thank you, Lord Selkirk...Mr. Robinson, do you have witnesses present, sir?

ROBINSON:
   Yes, my lord, I have forty witnesses ready.

POWELL:
   Well, Lord Selkirk, I see no reason why we should not begin to hear the case. Your witnesses will not be needed for a few days anyway. I will overrule your objection. Do proceed, Mr. Robinson.

ROBINSON:
>My lord, the presentation to prove the allegation of conspiracy, which is always, as you know, a difficult matter to prove in law, and demands an elegant containment of evidence, is particularly complex in this case because of the large number of witnesses. For that reason I suggest that the best person to examine the witnesses is Mr. Simon MacGillivray who is present in the court and prepared to undertake the examination.

SELKIRK:
>What are you asking?

ROBINSON:
>I am asking, Lord Selkirk, to have Simon MacGillivray conduct the examination of witnesses. As a Scottish peer, formerly a member of the House of Lords, you must have some comprehension of the Grand Jury system.

SELKIRK:
>I do, indeed, Mr. Robinson, and I have some comprehension of fundamental principles of justice. Is this a case, my lord, of the Crown against Selkirk or of the North West Company against Selkirk?

POWELL:
>Come, come Lord Selkirk, try to be a little tranquil. Of course this is a case of the Crown against Selkirk. This is not a matter of one party against another party, as you well know.

SELKIRK:
>Well then, my lord, if you let William MacGillivray's brother stand in for the Crown, you are admitting what all Upper Canada claims, that the MacGillivray family is the Crown in the Canadas. (Both Powell and Robinson intervene at once. Powell hammers the desk)

POWELL:
>Lord Selkirk. You must observe the order of this

court.

ROBINSON:
    I have never been so insulted in my life. How dare you say such a thing, and in this court...

SELKIRK:
    Mr. Robinson, I believe you are retained by the North West Company in one of your other capacities. Tell me if Simon MacGillivray is here as a friend of the court, as your witness, or as your employer.

ROBINSON:
    Objection my lord. Objection. I will not stand for this insult. Lord Selkirk is suggesting that I am a paid party of the North West Company.

POWELL:
    (Hammers the desk) Lord Selkirk, if you cannot conduct yourself with propriety in this court, I shall have to take sanctions against you.

SELKIRK:
    Mr. Robinson, you provided for the escape of every one of the murderers of innocent victims at Seven Oaks, and you did it by claiming that a dispute between parties where no law exists cannot be called murder.

ROBINSON:
    Objection, objection!

SELKIRK:
    Mr. Robinson, you freed cold-blooded murderers...

POWELL:
    Order! Order!

SELKIRK:
    You freed cold-blooded murderers because you said then, as you are trying to say now, the only law on the Canadas is the law of the North West Company. You said it. The courts helped you.

SELKIRK cont'd:
> The courts helped you release murderers, arsonists, kidnappers, thieves...

ROBINSON:
> My lord this must stop!

POWELL:
> Lord Selkirk, I may have to cite you for contempt of court. I will say no more for the present. You will all hear from me tomorrow morning when this court will reassemble.

SELKIRK:
> My lord?

POWELL:
> Lord Selkirk?

SELKIRK:
> Notwithstanding the outbursts in the court, we will serve notice that if Mr. Simon MacGillivray is considered as an examiner of the witnesses for the prosecution, we will object, formally in the strongest terms.

POWELL:
> Thank you, Lord Selkirk. I shall make my ruling. Depending upon it you may or may not object. I do not know what my ruling will be. I will give that, too, tomorrow. We will not proceed with this case until tomorrow.

SELKIRK:
> Thank you my lord.

POWELL:
> You do not look well, Lord Selkirk, but that does not permit you to engage in unrestrained and insulting behaviour in the court. The case is adjourned until tomorrow morning at ten.

(Lights down and out)

Scene Fifteen

(1818. Montreal)

LADY SELKIRK:
Are you sure the case won't be reopened?

HALKETT:
I am sure of nothing that relates to the harrassment of your husband. But when the Chief Justice barely referred to the irregularity in court and didn't mention the phrase contempt of court, it was plain they were skating on thin ice...

LADY SELKIRK:
Skating on thin ice, maybe...but we still had to sit through three days of witnesses lying through their teeth.

HALKETT:
Three days of witnesses and wholesale perjury couldn't put a complexion of conspiracy on our actions. The adjournment embarrassed Powell, but he carried it off like a master.

LADY SELKIRK:
There can be no justice here. Fifty-six people of the North West Company have been charged. After two years, only seven have been brought to trial. Every one a tragic farce. In the same time every single charge against us has been heard. I don't know how they can go on. Even the press is getting critical of them. Every charge against us so far thrown out, won acquittal, or stopped midstream by an embarrassed court - and still they persist. We can't be convicted. And they don't dare let any of their major offenders come near a court...they'll win against us. They won't rest until they get some convictions. Against the other side there'll be no convictions.

SELKIRK:
There is nothing left to do but to go to England.

SELKIRK cont'd:
>We'll see if there's a shred of justice left there.

LADY SELKIRK:
>Let the wicked flourish, Thomas. Haven't you learned yet the resilience of their power? They cannot - whatever they do - take our sense of right from us. No bestiality they commit does more than blacken their own reputation finally. Right can't always triumphant. Don't let them steal the last vestiges of your health, and our final years together. What can it gain you?

SELKIRK:
>It's not a matter of gain. Each of these cases, each escaped criminal is a grant of license to the North West Company to murder more settlers, to destroy the Red River Settlement and all it stands for. I work against that...

HALKETT:
>Thomas, you've done that work, and you've done it well. You've exposed the North West Company for the world to see. You've introduced civilization into the North West. There'll never be another Seven Oaks.

SELKIRK:
>I'm not so sure.

HALKETT:
>The interests of the fur traders have been saved. That's true. But the power of the North West Company itself has been broken - broken forever. Your shouts in court shouted down the last moments of North West Company despotism. But now you must stop. You must stop altogether. If you don't the only thing we can be sure about is your death. Nothing else.

SELKIRK:
>I know too well what you mean, John. We've broken the North West Company, so it's officers will

become land agents. From killing settlers with
the bullets of halfbreeds, they'll turn to breaking their hearts with the cost of land. I'm not
sure any victory's been won. I'm only sure greed's
beginning to change its direction.

HALKETT:
Perhaps your greatest courage, Thomas, and your
greatest folly, was to take on your own class and
think you could beat it.

SELKIRK:
I'm not through yet. I'll go to England to seek
justice for the settlers there. I'll try to
interest Wilberforce and some of the others in a
scheme for settlement without the use of land
companies. Such a scheme has the richest possib-
ilities of usefulness to the poor, to British
interests abroad, and to any future vision of
decent human community...

(Lights down and out on the last sentence)

Scene Sixteen

(1820. London. This scene was played with the Selkirk group on the upper stage, and with MacGillivray and Cameron and John Beverley Robinson sitting in very dim light on the lowest stage. When scene sixteen is over, light goes down on the Selkirk group and up on the MacGillivray group. He rises.)

LADY SELKIRK:
    Come now, look at the view. It's beautiful. You can see the valley and the people passing by the road. This fever, and the coughing fits shake you so that my own body feels wracked.

SELKIRK:
    The cough has abated a little these last days, from the air, perhaps, and the new tonic you managed to find. That's something to be cheerful about.

LADY SELKIRK:
    That and the news from Prince Edward Island just come, that's good news, surely to be followed by more.

HALKETT:
    What news is this? Something to lift our spirits?

SELKIRK:
    A letter from William Johnson at Prince Edward Island. Took scant three months to get here. A good report, John. We have, he says, the best settlement on the Island - all contented, happy, and thriving.

LADY SELKIRK:
    All we wanted done has been done there.

HALKETT:
    Contented settlers, loyal subjects, and proof settlement can work and grow.

SELKIRK:
> I know you both wish my peace of mind. But there's too much I can't seem to get my hand on...perhaps I've tried too much.

HALKETT:
> You wouldn't heed my words before we left Canada, and you haven't listened to anyone since. Do you rest? Do you sleep?

SELKIRK:
> I can't leave the job undone, John. I can't leave the settlers without even a pretence of protection. I dare not...can you imagine their fate.

HALKETT:
> The settlers are becoming more secure. Your drumming on the Colonial Office, your broadcasting evidence here is bearing fruit.

SELKIRK:
> I don't see it. Or am I being denied news again? Do you know something I don't know?

HALKETT:
> You aren't being denied news, Thomas. The last time I tried to spare you news, you made me swear. I've kept my oath. But yesterday, I received a communication, to me, personally, and I've held it only until now to think about it.

SELKIRK:
> Who is it from?

HALKETT:
> From the North West Company, indirectly.

LADY SELKIRK:
> Overtures?

HALKETT:
> Sent to me through Hudson's Bay contacts.

SELKIRK:
   Overtures from the Nor'Westers. That's something new.

HALKETT:
   MacGillivray wants to buy all your shares at the price you name. Terms include absolute guarantees for the settlers as you set out. If they want to move, MacGillivray guarantees to move them wherever they wish to go, free of expense. The final condition is that all prosecutions be dropped, mutually, and the slate wiped clean.

LADY SELKIRK:
   I said you've broken their hold. Here's proof. Now they came suing for peace. Here's a way, perhaps, to bind all up and get some peace of mind at last.

HALKETT:
   What do you think, Thomas?

SELKIRK:
   I think you're offering a counsel of despair. Put controlling shares in the hands of murderers and bandits? Should I, who led settlers into the jaws of famine and murderous slaughter, repay the settlers' courage and loyalty by feeding them blindfolded to their murderers?...Never. No. Those settlers will not be murdered or packed and driven from that place. We will be loyal to them and to the reputation of our cause. Only when the settlement is strong and the boats of settlers are arriving naturally to fill the land will the truth become clear to all. Then the evidence will be re-sorted. Then the world will see how a pack of murderers in the disguise of gentlemen and governors engaged in "liberal" conduct and trade, as they called it, ravaging the land, brutalizing the Indian, halfbreed, and white man alike - whoever they could bribe or coerce...I would change my decision for one person only in the world. But I don't think she will ask it...I will be dead soon. As somebody

or something I no longer matter. Everthing belongs
to them, and to the idea...a great idea which can't
be destroyed by breaking a little flesh.

LADY SELKIRK:
We cannot be put through worse than we have been
through so far. If we're to win, we don't stop
now. Do you believe the overtures, John?

HALKETT:
MacGillivray has appended a note himself which I
cannot but read as a retreat. They have lost much
and are in a most shaky position. The North West
Company cannot last long. Even the Royal Commission
which you forced, Thomas, declared the Nor'Westers
oppressive and criminal - when they finally got a
report in. Shareholders want profit, but they want
to be spared the sight of blood. They demand quiet
and orderly exploitation. The best oppression of a
people is peaceful oppression. Cracks are showing
in the North West Company. Rumour is that the
wintering partners - out in the field - are feeling
towards arrangements with the Hudson's Bay Company.

LADY SELKIRK:
If that's all true, we can wait a little yet.
There'll be no money. An immediate sale would
secure us, and I suppose MacGillivray knows it.
We've lost. But we've won a little, too, and
there's more to be won for the settlers and the
idea of the settlement. We will hold, John. That's
our answer to the overtures.

SELKIRK:
As you used to say in Canada, John, my class has
seen fit to punish me. Punishment by murder, by
perjury, by arson, by the terror of the Crown. I
fear they will grow used to that in Canada. They
permit it too easily. My class has achieved the
defense of its interests. They even got their con-
viction against me as soon as we left. Now they
come bearing offers of purchase. If I sell, they
can tell the world that I am not a bad, not an

unreasonable fellow, though misguided of course.
My class, having shown me they can only have one
interest, one common goal - profit and power - my
class will take me back, permit me a half-accept-
ance into their good graces. That's the morality
of my class. This new offer stinks more than anything else they have done. It shows they work out
their strategy down to the last small point. They
need me to surrender for their final victory, for
their historians who come after. But they won't
have my surrender. We will hold, John. But we
won't only hold. No. We will go on...even now
Miles Macdonnell is in Geneva recruiting for the
Red River. I must go to Geneva...I must get there
soon. We can't stop now, Jean. I must go to
Ireland, too, to help recruit there...there is much
to talk about and much to work out, much to do. The
stimulus of necessity has carried this great undertaking forward, in spite of all opposition. We have
always risen to the stimulus of necessity, have we
not, Jean? I must get to Ireland...I must finish
my pamphlet on the need...we can't stop now...we
must go on...Jean...Jean...

(Selkirk is wracked with a coughing spasm. He seems to
choke. Lady Selkirk and John Halkett move to him as
coughing ceases. They maintain a frozen pose as scene
shifts to the Nor'Westers)

Scene Seventeen

(1821. Montreal. The table looks like a table at a banquet or a board meeting. MacGillivray is upstage. The table is centre stage so that when he addresses what might be the shareholders he is addressing the theatre audience.)

MACGILLIVRAY:
    I was the first English clerk engaged in the service of the North West Company on its first establishment in 1784, and I have put my hand and seal to the Instrument which closes its career and name in 1821. The loss of the North West Company is a sad matter and one which grieves us all, for the company has written some of the noblest and most courageous pages in the annals of this land. Great names and great deeds went with the name, the North West Company. Its passing is much to be regretted, for with it has gone a spirit of enterprise and a spirit of self-dependence that will be hard to match anywhere. (Cries of here, here.) I'm happy to report to you that the merger with the Hudson's Bay Company - which wipes out our name - does not wipe out our being. Some of the best hands, Duncan Cameron, faithful servant, and Archibald McLeod, have gone into happy retirement. Duncan Cameron, indeed, has been raised to the position of member of Parliament for Upper Canada. (Shouts of here, here.) Alexander MacDonald has unfortunately been unable to find a suitable position with the new Company. But the rest have places of honour in the larger operation.

    I am told that nearly ten of our people who were so ruthlessly set upon by Governor Semple and his soldiers at Seven Oaks have been murdered in one way or another since the day of that unfortunate accident - I beg your pardon - that unfortunate incident. Proof again, that injustice against the North West Company goes largely unpunished since the advent of the settlers and the settlement. But we have begun, afresh, with a new slate. All litigation has been dropped, as you know, for most of the claims were exaggerated on both sides,. and the newly constructed Company would do ill to war within itself. The new Company, blessed as it is by Bishop Straughan, approved of by the speedily rising John Beverley Robinson, smiled upon by governments here and in Great Britain, can only flourish in the future as far ahead as the mind can imagine. For all the people involved share the same interests, and they are wise enough not to entangle with conflicts like those of the past. We have all learned a valuable lesson, and come out of it stronger than ever before.

And now, on a sadder note...we have been apprised of the recent death of Lord Selkirk of the Red River Colony. He was a man widely respected in some circles...and not so much in others. Whatever we may have thought of him, the past is the past. He may in fact be said to have been one of the authors of the merger of interests between the North West Company and the Hudson's Bay Company. To him we owe much of the strength that is present in the new Company. We deeply regret his passing. (Applause)

With regard to Lord Selkirk, I have recently received a letter signed by some people in Montreal and Toronto claiming to be friends of the widow of Lord Selkirk. Some of you may remember her. The writers of the letter suggest that we should raise by subscription from among the members of the Company money enough to build a cairn and raise a memorial to his Lordship's memory and work. I have written back on your behalf, declining the suggestion but promising to send the letter on to Mr. John Halkett who has travelled to the Red River where he is, I am told, putting the settlement in some kind of order. I suggested to him that the settlers, those of them who are left, being the chief beneficiaries of Lord Selkirk's largesse, would be the most fitting to raise a cairn and a memorial to his life and work.

I wrote to Mr. Halkett that they would be the people

who would want to undertake such a project and would feel sorely slighted if we were to intervene and by a greater show of wealth make their efforts seem timid or unappreciative. I told Mr. Halkett that, however deeply our feelings are moved at the memory of Lord Selkirk, we would not want to engage in the project and that, in general, we would not want to get a reputation for wasteful and showy benefactions.

(Lights down and out)